THE ICE IS NICE & CHEE-CHEE IS PEACHY

RICHARD H. HAVERMALE, JR.

DEDICATION

To the Almighty Lord Our God Creator of all things great and small; who is the True King of the frozen wasteland.

To the memory of the men of the Robert Scott party who lost their lives on their return trip after reaching the geographic South Pole.

To the memory of Roald Amundsen who announced to the world on March 7, 1912, his success in reaching the South Pole.

To the men of MCB71, the ICE Battalion, and the men of "Operation Deep Freeze".

To the US Navy SEABEE's who are marking the 70th anniversary of their establishment on March 5, 2012.

WARNING

This book contains material that may be considered rude, crude and socially unacceptable—nobody under 17 is allowed!

COURAGE---SACRAFICE---DEVOTION

CONTENTS

"To Strive, To Seek, To Find and not to Yield."
(Tennyson, 1842)

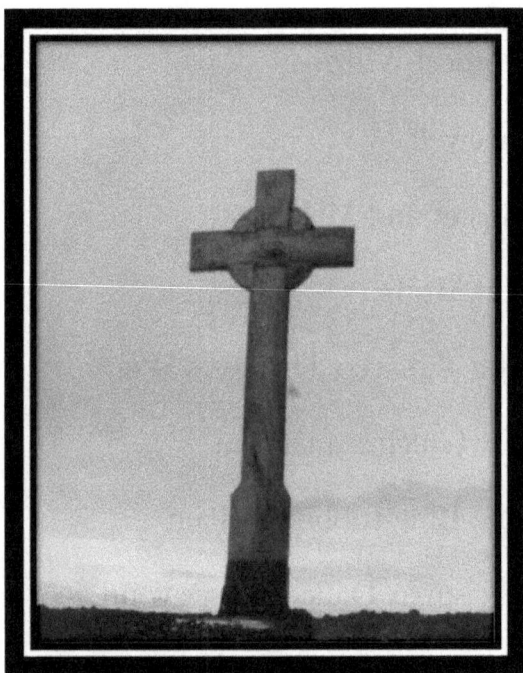

ACKNOWLEDGMENTS

I would like to thank Diane Havermale for saving all the letters I wrote to her from the ICE; without them, this book would not have been possible.

1 HEROES! VILLAINS!

Every man or woman was a hero and a villain at some point in his or her life. This is a story of me and the men of the United States Mobile Construction Battalion (MCB) 71, known then as the "The ICE Battalion", and our lives as heroes and villains in the frozen continent of Antarctica.

As children we have many heroes, one of my favorite was John Wayne. John starred in a movie called, "The fighting Seabees." I was nine years old when I saw this movie. I was so impressed with the Seabees, as a result, I asked God in a short prayer to let me someday be a Seabee.

Nine years later, at the age of 18, I joined the United States Navy in August of 1971. I had long forgotten about being a Seabee and was now thinking of being a Navy diver, mainly because being more mature, I no longer had a movie star hero, but one of flesh and blood. My new brother-in-law John (not Wayne), was a US Navy diver and living proof heroes do exist. In joining the Navy, I was on the road to becoming a hero, too.

Being a diver in the Navy was not easy. First, you must go through basic or boot camp, during boot camp you selected five job classifications that you might like. The job or rating as it was referred to in the Navy would be selected for you based on a classification test and the needs of the Navy. After being selected for a rate you, the Navy sent to a naval trade school, which you must pass to receive your rating and then request to go to diver's school. Being a diver in the Navy was a secondary job and anyone could do it-be they a cook or Seabee.

I followed this course. After completing testing in basic training, I met a counselor who told me I had a high mechanical ability and suggested that I go into that field. I had selected five job choices, they were; Molder, Damage Control Man, Aviation Mechanic, Builder, and Steelworker. As fate or God would have it, I was one of two trainees in my basic company selected to be a SEABEE! I was going to be striking for the rate of Steelworker—a childhood prayer fulfilled.

That tells you how I got started in the Seabees, so now let me tell you how the Seabees got started.

The Seabees were established on 5 March 1942, the purpose for their establishment was for the construction of bases and airfields during wartime and to defend what they build; hence came their motto, *"We build, We fight"*. The Seabees formed into construction battalions made up of construction workers from every field. They were given  the name Seabees from the "C" in construction and the "B" in battalion, thus the US Navy Seabees was born.

During World War II, the Seabees distinguished themselves in many ways, constructed, bases and airfields under impossible odds, and thus established their second motto *"Can-do."*

This "Can-do" spirit was what first sent the Seabees to Antarctica in the mid 1950's. Their purpose besides minor construction, included building and operating a nuclear power plant at McMurdo station on the coast, to making a deep-water wharf of hay bales soaked with water.

The Bee's also took equipment and supplies across the continent of Antarctica in bulldozers. An old sea story[1] states, that it was during this trip that Marvin Shields[2] lost his life by volunteering to drive ahead of the convoy, the self-sacrificing reason was that if he ran over a crevasse only he would be killed. For his act of selfless duty to his brother Bees, as the story goes, he received the Congressional Medal of Honor; which was untrue.

It was, however, with this equipment that the Amundsen-Scott station at the geographic South Pole-90 degrees south was constructed.

In the late sixties, it was discovered that the South Pole Station was sinking into the snow. This sinking was due to heated passageways and buildings melting into the ice under foot and sinking lower in the snow. This in turn caused air pockets to form overhead and the station was in danger of caving in.

In the early seventies MCB-71 was ordered to start construction of a new South Pole station. The new station was designed to eliminate the problem of sinking by the use of a geodesic dome and wonder arch.

The dome and arch would support the continuous buildup of snow that would eventually cover the structure. Entrance would be made possible by extendable tubes to the surface. Inside of this outer skin were buildings that were supported on stilts to eliminate heat transfer from the buildings, which caused the buildings to sink in the snow at the old South Pole in the first place. Construction of the buildings under the dome began in November

---

[1] a fairy tale that starts with, "Thwas ain't no shit."

[2] Marvin Shields did receive the Congressional Medal of Honor but for service in Vietnam; he was never in Antarctica.

1973. The men who constructed these buildings and the remaining wonder arch, worked in about the worlds coldest temperatures, with a yearly average of 46 degrees below zero.

The new (1975) South Pole station was less than one third mile from the geographic South Pole. The snow at the South Pole drifts North at a rate of 260 feet a year. The new station would, at this rate be within a half mile of the geographic South Pole for the entire 10-year expected life of the newly constructed dome and wonder arch. In February 1974, the Bee's had completed all of the construction for Operation Deep Freeze 74 and also 98 percent of the construction for Deep Freeze 75. The cost of this construction was more than seven million dollars that was funded by the National Science Foundation.

The dome was 164 feet in diameter and 52 feet high, the buildings within it were used for scientific spaces, living quarters, communications, and it had a library. It also had a galley (dining facility), club, and Post office. It housed 32 persons during the summer and 18 in the winter. Attached to the dome were a series of tunnels, made of wonder arch that had buildings under them. These buildings were used as workshops, labs, a generator plant and fuel bladders.

This story was of the men that constructed this station on one of the world's last frontiers, our lives and our insanities. The title of the book was also the saying of the ICE Battalion—it refers to our mission and our R&R (rest and recreation) in Christchurch, New Zealand.

"THE ICE IS NICE AND CHEE-CHEE IS PEACHY"

"MCB 71, Second to none"

2 FAREWELL

(Davisville, Rhode Island, late September 1973)

It was a cold day, but the sun was shining, trying to brighten the hearts of the men of MCB-71. For nearly six months, we would be away from our wives and sweethearts in the frozen wastes of Antarctica. On the ground, near the buildings and fence lines, were the last remnants of snow from three days earlier. The snow holds on for a last piece of life on the solid structures. It seems to symbolize loves-farewell, holding on until the last minute, knowing the inevitable would come. Farewell.

Those of us that do not have wives or sweethearts to say goodbye to, stand around in small groups. I was a member of one of these groups the other members were; Capt. Brillo, Hoombag Snagadag Bragg, Groucho Marx, Danks A lot, and Mountain. We were all steelworkers and we were excited about working and playing in one of the earth's last frontiers-Antarctica. I was the oldest member of the group at a ripe old age of 20.

Capt. Brillo got his name from Chief "Burnout"[3]. The name stuck after an in-ranks inspection in which the Chief was staring at Brillo's beard and dryly commented that his beard looked like a used brillo pad. Brillo was slender, nearly six feet tall and was an

---

[3] Real name was not used to protect the innocent-that is what we called him anyway.

American British citizen. He enlisted in the US Navy after having lived in California most of his life.

Hoombag Snagadag Bragg just took that name for himself. I have no idea why—except for maybe some bravado. We refer to him as Hoombag. He thought of himself as a dashing figure. He was not tall about five feet 9 inches with a full dark beard and a muscular build.

Groucho was his name simply because his last name was Marx—as in the Marx brothers from the movies. Although sometimes when we were bored, and we needed some action—we would piss him off by singing in a very irritating high-pitched voice his first name, "Roman"—ooooohhhhhh, "Rooomaaaan". He was tall and stocky with a butch haircut, rather dangerous looking, but was gentle as a lamb. I suppose that, was why, we teased him the way we did.

Danks and I were called by our last names. Sometimes the group called us brothers, because we lived less than a mile from each other in Phoenix, Arizona. Although, we never knew each other before we joined the service. Being called brothers always bothered Danks, because he thought himself superior to me, but I never let it annoy me. I even at times thought of him as my little brother.

Mountain was just that, for at first sight you would think he could kill you without batting an eye. I soon found out he also was a real gentleman, and a good friend; a real mountain of a man.

Brillo, Hoombag, Groucho, Danks, Mountain and I told jokes and talked to pass the time waiting for the plane to come. During the course of the discussion someone said, "It's always the same old shit, "Hurry up and wait."

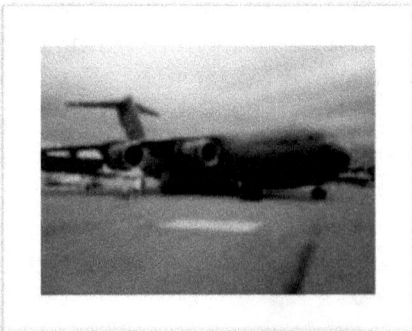

Finally the plane taxied up to our ramp, men said goodbye to their wives and sweethearts. It was one last embrace prior to entering the plane. The plane was a military C-141 transport; I could hardly wait to enter that massive pile of bolts. I had never been in a C-141 before so I had no idea of the joys awaiting me. First off, the plane had no flight attendants, bummer. I could live with discomfort but to make things worse the cabin was unheated and at 50,000 feet, I froze my koo-diny's off. I tried to console myself and thought that this would help me in preparing for "The ICE", but that did not work very well. Once aboard we were given small pieces of wax, to put in our ears because the plane had no insulation-the purpose of the wax was to be used as earplugs to help deaden the jet engine noise. Most of us put it in our ears, although one intelligent young man thought it was gum and promptly plopped it in his mouth and started chewing. I was told he thought it was gum to help overcome the air-pressure by chewing. We all had a good laugh at his expense. We relaxed as best we could; some slept, others read or played cards. I—was going to watch the flight across America, but to my disappointment, the plane only had two windows, which were on the exit doors near the tail of the plane. In addition, I was not impressed with the seating arrangements. The military plane had the seats facing the tail so in case of a crash, there would be a better chance of survival for the passengers and as an added benefit, we would not have to see ourselves die. The seats were a little cramped, however, the scrumptious, though stale, peanut butter and jelly sandwiches that were served for lunch made up for it. I found my thoughts drifting back to the last time I was in Davisville, R. I. It was over a year ago. Fate had ensured I was a Seabee; I reflected on how things started for me with my initial training in Davisville where I learned how to be a Steelworker in the US Navy.

"A" School, Davisville (Winter 1972) Rigging Rope Dopes

I remembered arriving in Rhode Island to attend Steelworker "A" School after being home for Christmas leave in 1971. I had completed boot camp in San Diego, California. I was excited about going to Davisville because the farthest East I had been was the Mississippi River when my Grandmother was dying and my father and I made a marathon drive from Phoenix, Arizona to his hometown in Quincy, Illinois.

I had managed to get from the Airport to the Naval Construction School, which was quite a distance from the Airport in Providence and settled into the barracks for construction school.

The room I was assigned to be in was small and it had a square table in the middle of the room surrounded by three double bunk beds and six wall lockers. I soon met the other construction apprentices with whom I would be going to school with for the next 12 weeks. We would be learning a multitude of ways of working with metal. Welding, sheet metal, soldering, fabrication of buildings and towers, metal landing fields, rigging, and rebar busting just to name some of the skills we would learn. I settled into my rack; (beds in the Navy were called racks) I was the last person to enter the room; I ended up with a top rack on the upper left side of the room. The day after I arrived, Bill Ferrier arrived whom I knew from basic training. Bill and I were the only sailors who were selected from basic testing to strike for the Seabees, we felt honored.

Bill was lucky. As it turned out the personnel office messed up and he was the last sailor ordered to Steelworker "A" school and the barracks manager decided that it was easier for him to keep all six of us in one room with Bill getting the other room all to himself. With our room, being so crowded the other guys would always ask Bill to use his room for a "Party Room." He was OK with that at first but he soon tired of it.

One night after we had just finished rigging class, I was studying and heard a commotion in the hallway. I went out to investigate and there was Cherokee banging on Bill's door screaming for him to let him, along with Wolfman and a couple of other guys in. Bill screamed back, "No, I want to be alone tonight." They kept banging when all the sudden Wolfman went to his locker and grabbed lighter fluid and then started squirting it under the door and lighting it on fire. The flames were starting to burn the actual door. The idiots; I had to do something but, what? Finally, I ran over, talked the A-holes into stopping with the flame-on trick, and put the fire out. Then, I screamed at Bill, that it was not fair. We were tired of our small room, and he should let us in; but he refused. "Alright Bill," I said, "Let me ask you one question, Do you have your window open?" He answered, "Yes, now go away." I turned to Cherokee and said, "I got a plan, get everyone's rigging ropes."

Our rigging ropes were ½ inch thick of manila line. The ropes were about six feet long; and on one end, we spliced the rope back on itself and made an eye splice; and on the other end a back splice to keep the rope from unraveling and then we cut the rope in half. With the two pieces in hand it was then that the instructor had us take the two cut pieces unravel them about six inches and we were taught how to make a short splice putting the now two ropes back together again. After we finished our ropes, we were allowed to take our ropes back to the barracks.

Upon Cherokees return with the six ropes, I instructed him and Wolfman to go up to the third floor tie the ropes together and attach them to a rack near the window. Then use them to crawl down to the second floor window of Bill's, go in and unlock the door. I really thought they would chicken out after looking down from the third floor and then come back and we all could get some peace. I stood in the hallway listening...listening, I did not hear them coming back? Then all of the sudden there was the sound of men struggling inside of the room and suddenly the door unlocked. To my surprise, there stood Cherokee grinning from ear to ear and when I entered there was poor Bill; tied up with the ropes.

Just then, my memories were interrupted by the sound of the C141 engines winding down and my mind went back to the present.

Magu Air Force Base, California

I could feel the pressure changing and we were landing. Just before the plane touchdown it began to sway wildly, I thought we were going to crash. Suddenly, we dropped and hit the tarmac hard, and a loud crack was heard from the rear of the plane. The plane then went back up in the air and then came back down again. Luckily, the pilot was able to regain control of the plane and we landed. As we taxied to the terminal, we were told that wind turbulence had caused the plane to set down hard on one wheel. We would have to disembark. We had landed at Magu Air Force Base in California for fuel but now we would be waiting for the repairs before we could continue.

I got off the plane, went into the terminal, and got a cup of coffee. Having some time on my hands, I decided to make a call, but I was not the only one with the idea. As I waited in line at the phone booths outside the terminal, I had a good view of Brillo and the other guys clowning around.

Brillo and the others were trying to stop cars, to take them somewhere to buy some "Coors" beer. Nobody was stupid enough to stop though. I assume that they thought they were a bunch of escapees from the nut house. Brillo was getting desperate, "Coors" at that time was a beer that was only available west of the Mississippi and because it had been over a year since he had that brand of beer. In his desperation, he walked out into the middle of the road and lay down, hoping to get someone to stop; it did not work, they turned the wheel and went slowly around him instead. It seemed like an eternity for the repairs to be completed but finally we loaded back into the plane for the next leg of our trip. Next, stop was Hawaii.

At our stop in Hawaii we had about two hours on the ground, I was fortunate enough to have my sister and her husband, John-you know hero-diver, meet me at the airport with her kids. John was stationed in Hawaii as a master diver. My sister and I had only a short time, but it was a blessing to have seen her and her family. The children were so big—I had not seen them for over two years now. My nephew, Brian 6, started crying and saying that's not my Uncle Dickie. (It's funny in retrospect that Brian was so tender hearted; later when he was all grown up; he joined the Army and was a Green Beret/Delta Force but that's another story.) Before I knew it, we were loading back into the plane again and we were back in the air, next stop, Pago-Pago.

Landing on Pago-Pago was interesting, you fly over a huge volcano and then swoop down and quickly land. The whole island was only four feet above the ocean except for the volcano. As we were on the tarmac, we saw the ocean waves splashing up! Then another re-fuel and we were up and away again. This was the last leg-next stop-Christ Church, New Zealand; affectionately known as CHEE-CHEE by the Bees.

3 MUSTER AND MAKE IT

Christ Church, New Zealand—CHEE CHEE

The engines of the C-141 wind down and we make a smooth landing on the tarmac of the New Zealand Army Airfield. We have been traveling now for over 40 hours and were we ever sick of it. We were more than ready to get out, but out we did not get. We were held on the plane for over an hour—Hurry up and wait! When they finally let us out, we were like a herd of wildebeests getting out of there. After clearing customs, we headed over to the New Zealand Army barracks. We would be staying in the New Zealand Army barracks for two weeks as we prepared for the deployment to the ICE. Only the officers and senior petty officers worked during the time of pre-deployment. We were left alone to get into trouble. *Muster and make it*; it was called. Every morning was roll call at 0800 hours—then the day was ours. Oh-Oh!

The barracks were simple affairs; rectangular wooden structures about 100 feet long and 25 feet wide with a door at each end, latrines and bays with bunk beds, which we called racks. I was berthed in a middle bay; I hurried in got a bottom rack and was quite satisfied. I thought myself smart by getting in quick. I lay down and rested tired from the trip—after some time the gang woke me up and by taxi, we were out to explore the city of Christ Church.

We ended up at a bar in the downtown area drinking Jelly Beans, which were made with ouzo (quite strong Greek liquor)—rumor was that you could get high because it was made with opium.

I quickly tired of this brand of fun and decided to strike out on my own. I walked about the town taking pictures. Then I went shopping and just enjoyed myself but I had no coat and it was getting cold. I went into a shop and brought a hat! It was not just a hat—it was a top hat. Yes—but not just your everyday black top hat. This one was special a perfect 70's style hat. It was beautiful with gold and orange colors in a giraffe pattern. I was something now! At six foot two inches tall, weighing in at about 150 pounds; wearing my plaid baggy pants and high heel shoes and topped by the hat of all hats--I must have been the picture of a man's man in the 70's— Damn I was proud of myself.

I headed back to the bar and made my grand entrance. The gang was roaring at my hat; by now drunker then skunks. I took it in good nature knowing they were secretly desiring my hat.

While in CHEE CHEE I learned from a US Navy publication that when we deploy we would arrive in McMurdo Station, Antarctica which was on the coast of the Antarctic continent.

"McMurdo Station was located on Ross Island in the McMurdo Sound of Antarctica and was one of the first stations built on the

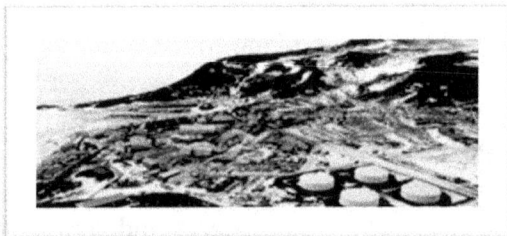

McMurdo

continent. Construction of it began on 20 December 1955, and the station became operational on 16 February 1956. McMurdo was first established as a logistical support base and its scientific role was added after."

"Scientific efforts in the McMurdo area began after 1956. Although biology and meteorology have been the primary scientific subjects the others are cosmic rays, ionospheric physics, geology, and glaciology." (Lewis)

"Since that time the Navy's role in Antarctica has been extended for an indefinite period. McMurdo has become the "supermarket" for other US Antarctic stations. Long-term occupancy made improvement of its facilities necessary. In 1962, a nuclear power plant was installed at McMurdo, making it the only Antarctic station using this type of energy source. A program to replace many temporary structures with fewer and permanent multistory buildings began during Operation Deep Freeze 1964 and was completed late in 1972. A plant to desalinate seawater and provide a freshwater distribution and sewage systems has made living conditions more comfortable. McMurdo was considerably larger than other US stations: a summer population of as many as 1000 persons was needed to receive and distribute supplies, to construct and improve facilities, and to operate the important air facility."

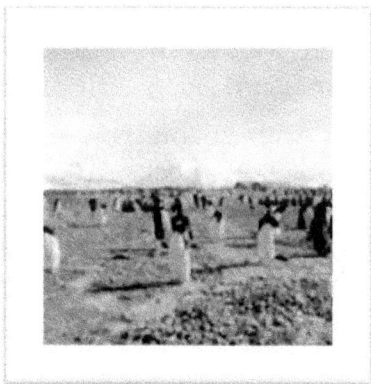

Emperor Penguins

"Southwest of the Naval Air Facility, a geometric pattern of semi-tabulate Jamesway huts insulated with fiberglass, and boxlike plywood butler buildings, painted orange, was built on Ross Island in the shadow of Observation Hill. Naval Air Facility McMurdo, with streets known as "Honeybucket Lane" and quarters called the "Hard-luck Hilton", evolved less than a mile from Scott's 1901-1904 quarters at Hut Point. For the edification of visitors, Seabees painted a large chamber of commerce style sign reading: (Navy, n.d.)

WELCOME TO MCMURDO SOUND PARADISE OF THE ANTARCTIC."

The time in CHEE CHEE passes quickly and before you know it the men and I of Mobile Construction Battalion (MCB) 71 prepared to load onto a C-141 military passenger and cargo plane. We would be flying from CHEE-CHEE (Christchurch, New Zealand) to our destination, McMurdo Naval Air Station, Antarctica.

We needed to load the plane—our personal things and equipment into the belly of the plane. Most of the men have brought few personal items for the six-month stay on the ICE. I have taken more than most; besides the usual footlocker, I also brought my guitar. Each man was now wearing long johns, which we called, waffle weaves because the cloth was in the same curvy shape as a waffle and we were carrying on with us the survival gear we needed when we arrived in Antarctica.

Bunny Boots

Our survival gear consisted of; one standard issue field jacket with hood and liner, one pant jacket (which we call many pocket) with liner; survival (bunny) boots, gloves with leather shell mittens and large furry mittens called bearclaws. The liner for the pants and jacket were made of a terry cloth material. Our Bunny boots were large white rubber boots with hollow pockets in the sides of the boot. These pockets of dead air space insulate the feet and there was a valve on the outside of the ankle of the boot, which allows adjustment of the air by twisting the valve open or closed. During the flight to the ICE we were instructed to leave the valves open to keep the boots from exploding from air pressure expansion.

At CHEE-CHEE it was a balmy 70 degrees Fahrenheit; when we get to the ICE it would be 15 degrees below zero. (Holy shit!) It was for this reason we would not put on the survival gear until we got closer to the frozen continent. After entering the plane, I soon hear the whine of the engines and feel the rumble of the plane as it rises into the air.

4 HUT MOTHER

1100 hours; 13 Oct 1973, McMurdo Naval Air Station, Antarctica

During the flight I talked and wondered what Antarctica would be like; was I prepared for this—Christ I had never even seen snow before I had joined the Navy; when they sent me to Rhode Island, for Steelworker training.

My thoughts were broken by the voice of one of my friends who was over at one of the two windows on the plane. He turned to me and said, "Hey, Havermale, Come here." It was Brillo. I got up and walked over to him, he says, "Look, we must be getting closer." I looked out the window and saw a giant Iceberg; I felt fear and at the same time wonder of at the majesty wroth by the hand of GOD.

I was scared, I thought I had a perfect right to be—I was a desert dweller; I had been most my life. My family moved from Quincy, Illinois to Arizona when I was two. I wondered if I could endure this cold. The sun was what I was used to. I thought of our survival briefing back in Davisville—where we were shown a film called the "Frozen Desert" because the snow at the ICE was so fine and lacking of moisture that it was like fine sand. They also stressed drinking plenty of fluids were necessary due to the low humidity. Having these two points in my favor I reassured myself that I had lived in somewhat similar conditions, and maybe I could survive the rigors of Antarctica.

Suddenly, I felt someone touch my shoulder, I turned, it was the Crew Chief; he tells us it was time to go back and strap in—for we were going to land on the ICE.

I sat quietly, waiting, wondered how it would feel to experience the coldest place on the earth. Just then, the plane bumps and slides on the ice; then slowly comes to a halt.

The door opened, I expected a sudden rush of cold air, but… there was none? I walked to the door bracing myself for the temperature change. I exited. I felt the brisk air, cool, invigorating, almost relaxing air, not at all like a shocking cold I expected.

I looked about; I hardly saw anything; the light was extremely bright. My eyes adjusted, white, white in every direction. It was stunning nothing but snow. I felt so desolate and lost and yet the beauty somehow made me feel one with Eternity. It was so cold that ice was forming all over my beard and face from my breath.

I look to right of the plane and there was a semi-truck and trailer. The trailer was red in color with the words "RED BEARDS EXPRESS" in large yellow letters. The driver walked to the rear of the vehicle opened the doors and motions to us to enter. I moved toward the trailer eagerly hoping the trailer would be warm. I was starting to shiver and feel a constant sucking of my body's warmth. As I entered the trailer, I saw the drivers face and realized that his name must be "Red" because of his flaming red beard. Red was smiling-enjoying our discomfort as if to say, "Welcome to Hell Froze over."

Inside the trailer were two rows of benches running along each side of the wall. I was the second man in the trailer, so I was able to get a seat. Most the men had to stand in a half crouched position and hold on to those who were seated to keep from falling during the ride to McMurdo Station. The cold, continued to draw from the core of my body, I started shivering uncontrollably. I was sitting next to Dino, who was in first. He was middle aged, tall with black thinning hair. He reached into a paper sack he brought on board and pulled out a half gallon of whiskey, put it to his lips and took a long draw. He shaked in an effort to shrug off the cold, turned and smiled at me, and said, "It's the only thing that cuts this cold." "Here, have some, it will warm you up." I take it, I felt the warmth flow from the inside to the outside—it felt great! I returned the bottle to Dino, and said, "Thanks a lot." Dino then passed the bottle around, and we all started talking, and suddenly we forgot the cold. As soon as the revelry started, we had arrived at McMurdo Station, Antarctica.

Our Hut

Red stopped the rig at the Fire Station located in the center of McMurdo. From there all our gear was unloaded and we were assigned sleeping quarters. We were

Jamesway

motioned toward a group of Jamesways. Our Hut was one of these Jamesways. Jamesways were half-moon shaped made of 2X6 boards and plywood. The roof was a half-round arc also of wood, from the inside it looked as if we were in an ancient sailing ship that somehow turned over on top of us. At each end of the building, which was about 60 feet long, were straight walls with an entrance. The entrance was especially constructed to keep the cold out the entryway has a double set of doors. It was about the size and shape of a phone booth; we refer to them as vestibules. The entire outside of the building and entrance ends were covered in a double canvas tent like material with about 1 inch of insulation in the middle, which made up the "hull of our ship". We were living in a tent at 50 below zero. What, were they nuts!

From the front door of our hut was the Ross Ice Shelf and to the left was observation hill. On our right was Scott's hut. Scott's hut was on a small peninsula about 100 feet wide and half a mile long jutting out in the ice. There was a small bay formed by the peninsula. This was where the dock was located but now all was ice and the bay would be that way until the first of the year. Scott's hut was an international historic site and was preserved as it was in 1904 when Scott used it as a staging area for exploration of the ice.

We go inside our hut it was freezing inside and start claiming racks. Inside the Jamesway were two sections divided by a partition wall on one side we had a kitchen supplied with conveniences for cooking; a hotplate, one pot, two butcher knives and a couple of large forks. The kitchen also had its own potbelly stove and on the other side of the partition wall was our sleeping quarters with its own potbelly stove. The stoves operated on a special fuel mixture that keeps the fuel from freezing. These stoves also had a square frame on the outside that was slotted to allow the heat out and kept people from being burned. It was very cold in the building but some of the guys with us were deployed here last year and knew how these stoves worked and fired them up. Soon the place was warm, well not freezing.

In a little while, the Chief came by to check on us. He saw that we had the heat started and was satisfied and turns to me and says, "Havermale you are the senior man here you are the **Hut Mother**." "*What!*" I started to object; I know nothing about this place most of these guys have been here one or two seasons and I asked, "*What the hell was a Hut Mother, anyway?*" The Chief replies, "It means you are in charge in this hut-you are responsible for everyone in here."

The building was not bad after it starts to warm up and you were wearing a coat. The kitchen was a simple affair with bar stools; small card table and couch. However, the floors were just plywood and very cold; we had to have our shoes on at all times to keep our feet from freezing. Some of the guys got a bright idea to store cokes under their beds but they froze solid and burst. Tomorrow we would draw supplies and stock our kitchen.

I went through the blue curtain used as a door to the sleeping quarters there were six double bunks along one side of the Jamesway and six along the other side. I had 24 souls in my charge, how was I going to take charge of these people? The men in my hut were a mixture of steelworkers and builders. I thought I could somewhat control the Steelworkers I knew but some of these Seabees were unsavory characters, and a few only came into the Navy in lieu of going to jail. I had particular concern with a Seabee named Mario. I tried to keep him from a fellow steelworker known by the name of Luigi. Mario and Luigi would get into some trouble; I could feel it in my bones, besides the cold, too.

As far as the bathroom went, we did not have one in our hut. We had to go to a latrine facility about 200 feet from our hut located on Honeybucket Lane. This building had water for showering and facilities for crapping. It was nasty to say the least and we were told to stay away from using the Flushies over at the permanent party building, which we called the hotel. This was a modern prefabricated building where the officers, Scientist and full-timers were housed. It also had the operations center for the National Science Foundation, Stores and Galley.

Our designated crappers were especially piquant with human waste. Toilets were simple affairs of a solid plywood bench with a toilet seat attached with five or six in a row. Waste was collected in a plastic bag put over a 55-gallon drum cut in half. Maintenance people regularly collected the waste and disposed of it in the McMurdo dump. The only good thing was it was so cold most the crap froze so it was almost breathable in there. If you happened to be using the crapper with six other guys at the same time it was…let's just say I timed my use of the facility to when it was not in use by others.

The hut was so cold Hoombag suggested we go to the club because it would take at least a couple of hours for it to get warm enough for us to take our outer gear off in the hut. Hoombag was the man with all the experience and the unofficial leader of our group; this was his second trip to the ICE so we followed him. He took us to the Ace-Duce club, we were not supposed to be there and the bartender was going to make us leave when a second-class petty officer not known to the others or me said he would sign us in as guests. We then soon become friends with all the petty officers there and we were never refused entry again.

The club had a large open area that was filled with tables and chairs. At other times, movies were also shown there. Against the wall was the bar and there was a pool room with a big picture window which gave you a wonderful view of the Ross Ice Shelf and Scott's hut. My friends started playing pool but I refused to play, it was not one of my talents. I just sat at the bar drinking a beer and looking out that picture window and tried not to show my fear to the others. My fear was that they would have seen the loneliness that was eating away at my insides. Outside the window was nothing, not a living thing and then a seagull flew into view. I thought this could be an answer from God telling me I was not alone. That he was and always would be there with me; no matter what. The seagull passed by and outside the window was nothing but rock and snow. Yet, that seagull was still in my mind. I thought all our lives

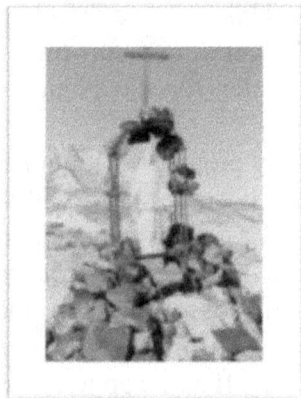

we live with other living things and tended to take life for granted. Here there was nothing but rock and snow, and nevertheless even here, life was holding on, at the very edge of existence. I wondered, "What in the HELL are we doing here?" I had not the answer, Oh the irony in that question was that man has asked that question of himself a million times in a million other times and places. However, maybe the answer to that question was in the question itself. "What in the hell are we DOING here?"

Pondering this question, I looked out on the ridge directly in front of the window and there at the top of the ridge was a figure with a small arch over it. I asked the bartender what it was and he said it was a statue of the Virgin Mary, "Our Lady of the Snows."

After a couple of hours we all went back to the hut and turned in for a long winters nap. The hut temperature was about normal now. We made our racks and settle in for some sleep but it was still light out and I ventured out for a look. In fact, the sun was only partially setting and seemed to dance on top of the mountains in the distance across the great Ross Ice Shelf.

It was the most beautiful sight, poetic, peaceful. I saw the simple beauty of the ice. I prayed and knew that HE IS. The chapel was not far from our hut and I went in and spend some time in HIS presence.

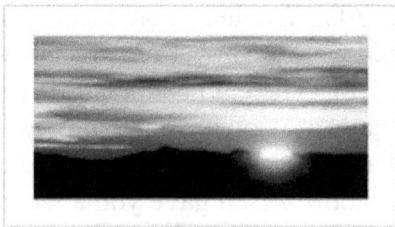

Upon my return, the Hut was dark. All I saw was the glow of the potbellyed stoves. All the lights had been pulled, we did have electricity and lights were simple affairs; just an electric wire hung down from the apex of the Jamesway with a socket and bulb and a pull string. I undressed and got in the rack.

No Heat!

I dozed off, I do not know how long I slept until I woke up; shivering. I got up and put on my survival gear. I was freezing-I went over to the stove in the sleeping quarters and it was cold. I do not know how it worked or how to get it started again. I then went over to check on each of the men. They were all cold too-teeth chattering cold. I got them up and had all of them put on their survival gear and then get back under their blankets, at least the stove in the kitchen was working and some of the heat was getting into the sleeping quarters but it was not enough. What do I do? I checked my watch it was 3 a.m., time for sleeping and I could not get help from the Chief then. I decide that what I needed to do was go over to the permanent station building, the building we call the "Hotel", find the person on duty and get some more blankets for the men.

I open the door and passed through the entry way and boom-I was blinded by the light-suns up 24/7. The air was dead with silence, so peaceful and tranquil. I felt one with eternity, I knew the sun would be up as I was leaving the hut, but I still expected that it would be a little dark and I was surprised when it was not. It was so light out and within the hut; it gave no indication of any light outside. I then thought, how ironic, at home people have artificial light and here at the ICE we lived in artificial darkness.

I headed on over to the Hotel and started looking for the person on watch. Finally, after what seemed like an eternity I found the watch desk. I went over introduced myself to the person not much older than myself on watch with dark straight hair. I explained that the heat had gone out in our hut and that I needed extra blankets for my men. He agreed but stated, "Sorry I am not authorized to give you blankets." I was sure he thought, "It was not my problem, I do not care." I pleaded, No that did not work.

Then, I got tough, although he must have felt safe, because he was looking at me through a window cut in the wall and behind a desk. Suddenly, I jumped through the window, grabbed him by the shirt, and pulled him partway through the window to me. I had an iron grip on him, being a steelworker I could easily pick up a quarter inch 4x8 foot steel plate and move them for construction and I was

21

not letting go of him. I told him with my face two inches from his; that if I did not get the blankets I was going to beat him silly. I would then take the blankets and that I would point him out so that every Seabee who saw him, would also, kick the shit out of him. He looked at me, trembling and said, "OK...OK", he quickly opened a closet and gave me the blankets and stated, "Is there anything else, Sir." I said, *"No, Thank you very much."*

I quickly made my way back to the hut, wrapped each man in a blanket, and ensured that they were OK.

The next day we got the stove fixed, but best of all Groucho worked in supply and stole mummy sleeping bags for all of us to ensure our survival should it happen again. I was uneasy with the theft but felt that it was justified under the circumstance, after all I just threaten a man and would have beat the total shit out of him the night before if he hadn't given me the blankets.

October 18--Work Details

Most of the Steelworkers and I were assigned to shoveling snow that had accumulated from the winter. As you worked, it was so ice-cold that frost formed on your beard, face and hair from the vapor of your very breath. Living there, I could really reflect on the statement: "God is closer to you than the very air you breathe". Being there gave new meaning to that. Your breath was always with you; you could not escape it; even if you tried. Your breath almost caressed you as you went about your day. I thought, *"Are we really loved that much?"* and then I reflected on John 3:16 from the bible and it seemed to make more sense to me.

> John 3:16: "For God so loved the world that he gave his one and only Son, that whoever believes in him shall not perish but have eternal life."

The work was hard and exhausting and we had to stop frequently. During breaks if the Chief did not observe us, we would play. We were like children in grown up bodies. I started to look for Danks, but could not find him. Then all of the sudden I found him, he was sitting in the shade of an ice shelf that formed a mini cave and fortunately he had not seen me. I was playful, snuck over, standing as silently, and stealthy as I could just above his cave; I then jumped as hard as I could on the ice shelf collapsing the whole thing on him. I tumbled down and we both scuffled like kittens; then busted out laughing. Then, it was back to work. We had to stop occasionally due to sweating. We were instructed that the easiest way to freeze was to get sweaty and then have the sweat ice up on you. We took advantage of this fact at every opportunity.

While we were shoveling, we found some small plastic containers with magnesium used in some welding techniques. We lit them and watch as they quickly sunk down through the ice. I turned to Danks and said, "*I wonder how far they went.*" He responded with, "Well I am sure as hell not going to dig to find out!" We laughed and shoveled some more. After we worked at least 12 hours, we were given some time off. I went over to the exchange and bought a souvenir tee shirt with an emperor penguin and the words "Operation Deep Freeze". I loved that shirt; it has long since deteriorated and was thrown out.

When I got home that night, I was making myself a peanut butter and jelly sandwich; I did not know what to do with the cans of jelly and peanut butter I had just opened. I finally worked up enough courage to ask Brillo what to do with it because we had no storage supplies to preserve food.

To which Brillo replied, "Just set it behind the bar"

To which I replied, *"But, the bugs will get it"*

Then very dryly Brillo said, "Havermale, just leave it anywhere."

I started to object but before I could say anything, he said, "Have you seen any bugs?"

"*No.*"

"Well if you do, catch it, and they might name its species after you!"

Later that night a few of the guys went over to the local bar but I didn't feel good and went to bed early.

October 19--Illnesses; injuries and insanities.

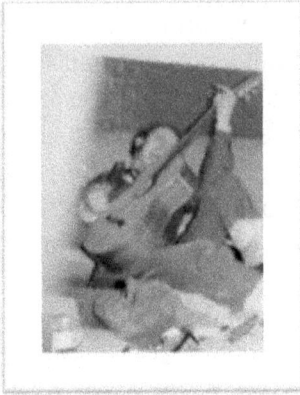

BRILLO

The next day began early; I was feeling a little under the weather and decided to go over to the sick bay at the end of the working day. I was given quarters for 24 hours and told to rest. On the way, back I started to notice that it was common for people to become strange, weird or maybe a little insane. For example, there was a very big man who had "wintered over" or spent the last 6 months in darkness at the South Pole. I thought his appearance might have described his mental condition; he had completely shaved his head but left on a six-inch full beard. Another guy I observed was carrying a Raggedy Ann Doll around with him, I was later told he even eats, sleeps and shits with Raggedy. Dude...now that was "Narly" (70's slang for cool). By the time, I got back to the Hut I discovered that most of the guys had left for the bar. Good I needed to get some rest. The next day even though I was sick I got up to get the men out to work for the day. I went over to Brillo's rack and noticed he had a huge knife from the kitchen stuck in between the wood frame of the Jamesway and the tent material. I had a hard time getting Brillo up. I talked to some of the guys and they told me Brillo must have drunken a case of the local beer last night. O'Shit! Rumor had it that the beer "Busch" which claims to be especially brewed for "Operation Deep Freeze" was rumored to have just a hint of formaldehyde in it to keep it from freezing and if you drank too much you might

24

experience hallucinations. Anyway, Brillo was out for the count. Finally, with help I was able to get him up. *"Brillo,"* I asked, *What's up with the knife?"* He said, Wow, Man-last night some little green man came into the hut and he came over to my rack, grabbed the rail, pulled himself up to eye level with me, and then moved his eyebrows up and down staring at me in an evil way. I got the knife just in case he came back. *"OK, Brillo-now it is time to go to work."* We got Brillo together and out the men went. At last, I went back to bed thankful to be on quarters for the day's temperature was going to be 80 degrees below zero.

I soon was asleep and hours later in came Brillo and he was trying to crawl into bed and he was having a difficult time getting in his rack; he had a top rack just like me and he just could not get in it. I said, *"Brillo, what's wrong?"* It was difficult to get him in the rack; I actually had to pick him up while he moaned in agony.

I said, *"Brillo, you sick too?"* He said, "No", "I am frostbitten" weakly. I said, *"Where?"* He could hardly say it, "I am frostbitten in my peter"

I shouted. *"What?!"* *"You frostbit your dick"* *"Come on?"* *"How the hell did you frostbit your dick?* It was difficult for him to talk; but finally he said, "Well I took a piss and left my zipper open and didn't tuck my boy back in my waffle weaves." "We worked for 2 hours straight and when I went in to warm up next to the potbelly stove I felt a searing pain in my peter and fell over." I did not believe him I thought it was bullshit—I thought no one could be stupid enough to have frozen their dick. I had to confirm this. I got up, got dressed sick and all. I marched over to the sick bay. I asked, *"Hey did some dipshit just come in here with a frostbitten dick."* The corpsman was laughing and said, "Yes and if he didn't come in when he did we would have had to amputate." *"Holy, shit"*—I fell down laughing.

When, I finally got back to the hut Brillo was asleep. I got up in the rack and I could not sleep even though I was exhausted, every few minutes I would start laughing all over again with thoughts about Brillo's accident.

The next day the dispensary declared me fit for duty and as soon as I got to work, we got a gale condition warning, which means we had to stay inside our hut. The Chief came by and presented Brillo with a little sweater made to cover his penis. To add insult to injury he made a big deal about presenting it to him. I took a picture of him wearing it--but there are just some pictures you never want in your head and for that reason; I am not including it in this saga of the trials and tribulations of Antarctic life.

As long as the Chief was there, I decided to ask him, if there was any wildlife at the South Pole; which we would be deploying to soon. He said, "No except that; you do have to look out for the Snow Snakes." I said, *"Snow Snakes?"* Then I said something dumb, *"I guess this place is like the desert, with snakes and all. Are they poisonous? Do they have fangs?* Then the Chief let me have it, "No, but if you are not careful, they will crawl up your ass and freeze you to death." Boy was I embarrassed but we all had a good laugh.

During gale conditions your mind got a little bored-There was no "Oprah" there and you tended to do stupid things.

For example, we had a huge club in our hut and I decided to go ringing doorbells on the second day of the gale with it. I went over to the next hut, started beating the outside of the hut with the club, and then ran back into my own hut.

While trapped in the hut some of the guys there were talking and they mentioned that Lipton's tea when it was burnt smells just like marijuana. I could not believe it; the next thing you know I was running back to my footlocker. I knew I had a pipe in there somewhere. Yes! I loaded it up with Lipton's and lit it. Tasted like pure shit but yes it did smell just like marijuana. Brillo and I were going to have some fun with this.

At lunch, we took my pipe with us over to the galley and we were eating slowly waiting for our victim. Then he came in, Mr. Winterover. You know the guy with his head shaved who wintered over stares at walls and things like that. He sat a few spaces down from us. Brillo and I watched him as he was eating soup like an "animal." Staring at the wall with his face about four inches from the bowl and eating quickly, one spoon after another; just staring at the wall. I pulled the pipe out, lit it, and took a big drag; held it in my lungs then let the smoke out. Then, I passed the pipe over to

Brillo, who did the same. The smoke drifted over to Mr. Winterover, all the sudden he stopped in mid stroke with the soup, sniffed, and then sniffed again. Slowly his head turned our way and he sniffed one more time. Then he dropped his spoon, jumped up and ran over to us like a kid. He said to me, "Hey, man is that shit" I said, *"Yah it's some Maui Wowi."* He said, "Holy crap man how did you get it here, with customs and all." I quickly said, *"Brillo here just hid it in his jacket."* He was rubbing his hands together and prancing.

"Hey man you don't mind if I take a hit." "Like man I ain't had any shit for 18 months." I said, *"Sure, here you go."* I handed the pipe to Mr. Winterover, he greedily grabbed it, put the pipe to his lips taking a draw bending his whole body backwards with the draw, then he took two more deep draws rolling his eyes back in his head, breathed out and said to me and Brillo, "Man, that was the best shit I have ever had!" Brillo and I could hardly contain our laughter.

After lunch we decided that it would also be fun to walk through the officer's quarter's area on the way back to the hut. It was interesting to note doors would open people would sniff through the crack in the door but nobody came out of their rooms.

On the third day of the gale, I ventured out and slipped down to the chapel, which was not too far from our hut I would just sit there and talked to God or played the organ. By the end of the third day, the gale lifted. When we went out to work, we saw the Gale had deposited 10 feet of snow, which we had to dig off.

One of the favorite things to do while you were there was to do some trading with the Kiwi's (New Zealand Army personnel) I traded my Navy white hat for one of the New Zealand Army hats. We both thought we got a good deal. Also the New Zealanders were a friendly lot and decided that after the gale it was a good time to show us real football (Rugby) they explained that it was just like American Football however there were no rules. I thought that was a mistake to put it that way.

For Mario, Luigi and Company then took full advantage of the opportunity to beat the hell out of the Kiwi's. Yes not only did the Bee's win the game but the Kiwi's suffered casualties: One broken jaw (slugged); some busted ribs (kicked) and a broken leg (piled on). The poor Kiwi's never had a chance.

In addition, after the gale Groucho and I decided that with the weather being nicer it would be a good time to go down to Scott's hut, built in 1902 for his expeditions. We found a dead seal outside the hut from that timeframe. There were three crosses commemorating men who had lost their lives here within sight.

Recently British journalist Ben Fogle gave the following report on his visit to Scott's Hut for the 100th anniversary of the hut and here is a short extract of his article on the experience.

"The first thing I noticed is the odour. Even though your senses are numbed by the cold, it hits you hard, because in Antarctica there is generally no smell. Aromas of old leather, pipe smoke, wood and horses still linger – along with a deep, powerful musty smell I later discovered was blubber.

The outer door leads into a covered porch. Old wooden skis are propped up along the corridor leading to the stables where Oates had tended the expedition's Siberian ponies. Large slabs of seal blubber, which were used for lamp fuel as well as food, are piled high in a corner.

Everything has been frozen in time; nowhere else on Earth can you taste history like you can in this weathered little building. It's as if the last occupants simply upped and ran, leaving their socks and their jumpers, their books and their coffee cups. The kitchen is still fully stocked." (Fogle, 2011)

October 21--"We dine like Kings"

My immediate supervisor was Steelworker Second Class Bucky. Bucky was a man's man. He was of average height and stocky. In addition to being a steelworker, Bucky was also a Navy Diver (I heard he had the world's record for the coldest dive) and a locksmith. The men in my hut tired quickly of the issue peanut butter and jelly and had convinced Bucky to help them get some real food and this was where Bucky's skills as a locksmith came in.

Saturday night Bucky and a few of the thieves in my hut came busting in laughing and carrying cases. It appears with Bucky's help as an expert locksmith they had broken into the McMurdo Stations freezers and stole 29 pounds of steaks, 30 Cornish game hens and cases of lobster tails and other sundry foodstuffs.

The cry went out, "Tonight! We dine like Kings."

I was a little perplexed. *"Bucky, why do they have food in a locked freezer if it is colder outside then it is in the freezer?"* I asked. His answer was that McMurdo would during the summer months get just over freezing and food has to be kept at a constant temperature. He asked me if I had been to Scott's Hut and I said, *"Yes"*, "Well" he said' "When you went over there did you look outside and find a seal that Scott's men killed to eat outside the hut and did you notice that it has partly rotted from the couple of weeks it was over freezing." He said, "That seal has been rotting just a little every summer for the last 80 years."

"Well" I said, *"I really don't think it was a good idea to steal this food"* and I refused to eat it. However, after the steaks started sizzling and the lobster was boiled and bathed in butter; my stomach said, *"Yes"* but my mind said, *"No"*. In the end, my stomach won.

After the feast I said, *"Now what are we going to do with the rest."* "No problem, Bucky said, "For the time we are here it will never get above zero." "We will have time to eat it; until then we will store it in the kitchen entry way." We locked the outside door and whenever, we wanted to eat, we just opened the inside door and grabbed it. Just like an upright freezer at home.

Ass Packing Party

An ass packing was an initiation rite levied on persons who have never been to Antarctica. There was no ceremony; there was no fun, except for the packers. The person was grabbed by several men dragged outside, stripped naked and buried in the snow and left that way to dig their own way out. Afterwards, they were given a blue ribbon strip 6 to 8 inches long of plastic engineering tape to attach to their uniforms as proof of receiving their rite of passage and that they had been reborn as members of the emperor penguin's court. After dinner the mob grabbed me and started to take me out to the snow for an ass packing but it was decided not to because I just got over being sick. Brillo's packing was also waived due to his resent frosty experience. However, seven other guys were showed no mercy; two of them were pulled out of their beds asleep before the ass packing frenzy stopped. I thought the guys were also getting a little bored and this was their entertainment.

October 23--White Out

During a "white out" the weather was strange. Coming back from the head (bathroom), Brillo, Danks and I looked up at Observation Hill and watched in awe as a mist came up over the mountain, then ran down the mountain like water. Then the mist rather quickly raced down the mountain and hit us. The wind was so strong we had to walk into the wind at a 45-degree angle with our hands daggling down missing the ground by about six inches. We nearly lost our hats and towels, which we had wrapped around us. I had never seen anything like it in my life, it was frightening like in an end of the world way.

When the "white out" ended I was assigned to drive a truck on the snow. It was interesting because I had never driven on snow or ice before. In addition, I was told the truck had no brakes. I was stuck going up a hill to the nuclear power station and the tires of the truck kept spinning and we were sliding backwards, too make matters worse there was a sheer drop off on the passenger's side. One of the guys in the back of the truck jumped out in fear and decided to walk. Adjusting the amount of gas I gave to the truck, I finally got the truck started up the hill again and I dared not stop. Unfortunately, the recent jumper, which was up ahead, was in my way. I could not stop, he saw me coming and ran until finally he had to jump into the snow bank to avoid being clipped by the truck. My concern was the truck would slide back off the cliff and we would all be dead; making it impossible for me to stop.

Later that night the sun was up and warm, it was at least plus 10 above zero. I had acclimated to being cold and found that I was sweating at that temperature and was able to go shirtless and felt fine. However, the next day was freezing and windy. When the wind was blowing it got so cold in our hut, we saw our breath.

October 26--The Grass of God

The next day I was very troubled; I heard some of the guys were smoking marijuana in the hut. I went over to the Chapel office and talked to the chaplain, I told him about the men in my hut smoking grass, and that I was concerned. He told me that it was my duty to report these guys if I catch them smoking grass/weed, etc. I was shocked, it took a great deal of moral courage to do that, and at 20 years old my moral courage was-let us say underdeveloped.

I was sure they did inhale. I never participated for I had taken an oath to myself that I would never do drugs; however, I did not take an oath not to be around those who did. I would had been a very lonely man if I did avoid those who did drugs; for everyone I knew was doing weed.

That may be the reason why the world situation seems to be getting worse today; maybe it was the Grass of God. It was the seventies, drug testing was unheard of, and some of the leaders looked the other way or worse condoned it.

I went in and I told the guys in the hut that if I catch them smoking weed, it was my duty to report them. It hurt my heart to say it and I had a feeling that they were not receptive of the word of God; I had just received from the chaplain.

The next day my courage wavered and I told the guys that I needed to rethink this whole dope smoking thing. In addition, I could not stand it that the guys were avoiding me like the plague; they were colder to me then it was outside. Moreover, the night before I got my ass packed, vigorously, and it seemed like it was a warning!

October 28--Laundry Babies

Saturday morning Captain Brillo and I went to turn in our laundry. It was indeed a luxury to have someone do our laundry. When we go to the South Pole we would not have that luxury and we would have only one washer for over 100 men to do their own laundry. I had a feeling that some people would choose not to and get pretty ripe while we were at the geographic South Pole.

While we were waiting in line to give the laundry personnel our laundry, we got bored and started play fighting. It was starting to get a little rough. Amazingly, it was like a bar fight out of an old western movie. Laundry personnel and those waiting in line just stared at us; it was as if we were all acting our parts in an old western script. No one intervened or tried to stop us; I guess they were waiting for the Sheriff to arrive and stop the fight; however, there was no Sheriff. Game on! I grabbed a big safety pin; about 6 inches long from my laundry bag, I opened it and pretended I was going to stab Brillo. I was really getting into my part in the western bar fight scene. Brillo then took his big bag of laundry swung it and knocked me over. I scared the shit out of myself when I almost accidently stabbed him, so I threw the pin away. He took full advantage of the lull in the fight, grabbed a water fire extinguisher off the wall, and started pumping the water from it into my ear. I broke free, grabbed the extinguisher turning it upside down, and emptied the remaining water all over him. Game over, I won. Laughing we then cleaned up the mess we had made and turned in our laundry as if nothing had happened and just like in those old western films, after the fight nobody said a word and I thought I heard the

"Saloon piano player start playing "Ragtime" on his piano again."

5 TOBACCO THROWERS WAR

Just another workday for us here, however, someone typed up a list of all of the Benefits of Antarctica and posted it on the bulletin board.

Benefits of Antarctica

- Where else can you go in the world and get to piss in a funnel that drains into a fifty-five gallon barrel?

- Where else can you go and have daylight all hours of the clock?

- Where can you go and not be bothered by women who just want to spend your money?

- Where can you go and be able to shit in a plastic bag which is half full or better and when you sit down you feel something touch your ass?

- Where can you go and only take only one shower a week and when you do the hot water is cold or not there at all?

- Where can you go and have very little communications with the outside and States?

- Where can you go and not be bothered with the problem of mail?

- Where else in the world can you go and have a whiteout with no warning at all?

- Where else can you go and be so isolated and not be bothered with the squeal of car tires and pollution of the big cities?

- Where in the world can you go and not see any trees or plants?

- Where can you have such enjoying evenings on weekends as we do here?

- Where else can you sit hoping for mail and finding out that Broke-Dick Airlines failed to make it?

- Where else can you go and spend four enjoyable Holidays all in five months?

- Where else in the world can you live in such mansions as we do?

- Where else in the world can you be free from humans and mother nature?

- Now really why and the FUCK are we here on this place when God didn't put us here to begin with? If we were supposed to be here then we wouldn't have had to fly down here on Broke Dick Airlines. Think about it....

I obtained and retained a carbon copy of the original prose. I had the keen sense to save this Shakespearean beauty for your enjoyment.

I was assigned to detail in the carpenter shop which was a much warmer experience than usual, however after lunch we were assigned to loading vans on sleds with a crane so the plane could pick it up to go to the Pole. It was interesting because in reality we were on the ocean. It was frozen six foot thick and the ice was the most beautiful color of blue. You could almost see through it. I swear I saw movement under the ice. After we finished loading we had a slack period. I turned around and everyone was gone. I noticed they had run into the crane, which was heated, and locked me out. So, I laid down on the ice and started to sleep. All of the sudden snowballs started hitting me. I retaliated but to no avail—I sucked at throwing snowballs. I was a fricken desert dweller. I had to retreat. Those snow bunnies were creaming me so I had to use vile trickery. I ran in and threw a couple of snowballs and then I took off with Groucho on my tail. I ran to where I had several snowballs prepared for use and when I got to them, I started to bombard him.

After work, in the evening for entertainment, we watched a movie for Halloween; I think it was Cat Ballou.

The next morning we were woken up by the chief banging on the shit can because we overslept. We quickly got dressed and that day I worked out at the vans again. My crew and I had to wait an hour for another crew to show up and froze our asses off. The temperature that day was 50 below zero.

We ended up at the club that night. I had three Busch Barbarian beers and found out I could not read the mail I got that day. I could not figure out if I was drunk or if the formaldehyde was getting to me. After we got a few beers in us, we decided to go sliding down the hills near Scotts Hut on large pieces of plastic. I had a blast because I have never been sledding before—even though it was 50 below zero. It's funny I didn't feel the cold. Do you think it was the beer?

Early November--Banana Sledding, Seals and Skua Gull fishing

On the ICE there were not a lot of categories of entertainment. There was no TV or radio and guys spend a lot of time looking at ways to entertain their selves besides working 12 hours a day. To beat the boredom some of the guys have drawn a small circle on the kitchen door to use as a target for knife throwing contests. I thought more than one Seabee considered his self a full pledged James Bowie.

Scout Memorial Cross Observation Hill Frank Debenham's 1913 photo of the cross

The other day I developed a trap for the amusement of the guys in the hut. I pulled one of the light strings up and replaced it with a string to a bag full of Styrofoam balls so when the string was pulled the Styrofoam balls would fall on you instead of the light coming on. With the sun being up 24 hours a day, guys would have four or five hours to get themselves into trouble. One night Hunsucker and I decided to hike to the top of Observation Hill. It was a hard climb straight up. He was physically stronger than I was (smoker) on the climb and I suffered but the climb was worth it. "On top of observation hill was a 12 foot cross of Australian Jarrah wood which was erected in 1913 in the memory of Scott's polar exploration party that lost their lives finding the South Pole. Etched on the upper limb of the cross are the names: Scott, Wilson, Oates, Bowers and Evans. Beneath was carved A few lines from Tennyson: "**To Strive, To Seek, To Find and not to Yield.**" (Lewis, 1966)

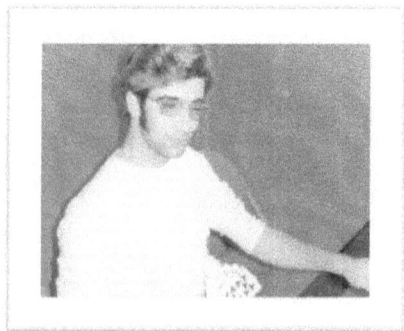

BUCN Jimmy Grace--Royal Flush

Besides hiking guys also played cards to relax—Jimmy Grace came over the other day and was dealt a Royal Flush. I took a picture of it because I was thinking it might have been the first; I mean what were the chances of getting a Royal Flush anyway and what were the chances of getting a Royal Flush in Antarctica! I really like Jimmy he was a faithful catholic here and a real gentleman and he would eventually be the Godfather of my firstborn daughter.

The temperature was getting warmer, the other day it was a +22 and I worked outside without my coat. We would soon be deploying to the geographic South Pole so we had to step up our outside activities during our limited free time.

I went sledding using a banana sled for the first time with Luigi and some of the guys. We would jump in the sled, which was for all intents and purposes impossible to steer. It was designed to be pulled to carry supplies. The game was to point the sled at a small knoll at the bottom of the ravine and try hitting it and jumping it. It was pure adrenalin. For a first timer, I was able to hit it perfectly making the farthest jump and I landed without breaking my neck. Dragging the sled back up the hill was hard for the slope was steep.

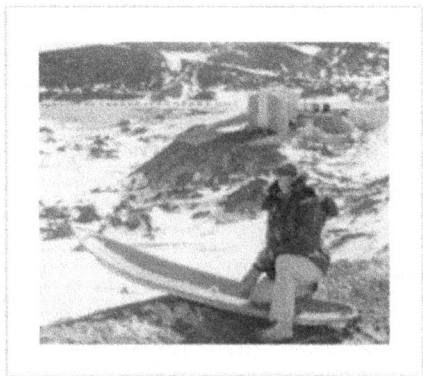

"Me" SW3 Havermale Banana Sledding

Luigi told me that this was tame compared to yesterday when he and Mario ventured out onto the ICE shelf to go seal riding. Yes, I said seal riding. I did not believe it until they showed me the pictures. These seals were about the size of a small horse. The picture showed Luigi riding the seal bareback with his feet about 6 inches off the ground with the seal trying to bite him. Regulations also strictly prohibited (I don't think that was a deterrent to Mario, Luigi and company anyway) us from going out on the ice due to it was the killer whales season for hunting for the seals on the ice.

Guys frequently do strange things in strange places. I heard of a guy who brought his fishing rod and reel here and instead of normal fishing he went for strange fishing. As the story goes and this "ain't no shit," was that, the guy attached a steak to the line and then threw the steak in the air which was grabbed by a skua gull. The gull refused to let the meat go and gave this angler the best sport fishing he ever had.

Another tale we were told was that Seabees and Coasties (US Coast Guard) don't mix and that there have been several memorial fights. One year I was told the Seabees actually chased the Coasties back to their ship, went on the ship, and started a party on it and the Seabee Commander had to go down there and ask the men to give the Coasties their ship back. I don't believe it but you never know. I mean who would believe someone would frostbite his dick like Brillo.

The next evening I was sitting down writing a letter when Groucho and Brillo came in. Groucho also had with him a cardboard box, which he seemed very proud of, so I inquired about it. He said, "It's a case of Chesterfield cigarettes."

I said, *"Why in the world did you buy a case of Chesterfields? You don't even smoke that brand."* "Well, I got the whole case for only 90 cents", he proudly said. I interjected, *"What? Where did you get that many cigarettes for 90 cents? What's wrong with them?* To which he responded, "I got them at the exchange, they were old so they just sold them for 90 cents to get rid of them. Here try a pack."

I opened the package and pulled a cigarette out, but before I got it up to my lips all the tobacco fell out on the floor. I looked at Groucho out of the corner of my eye and said sarcastically, *"How are you supposed to smoke 'em when the tobacco falls out?"*

"O' I already figured that out, hold the cigarette pack on its side and put the cigarette in your mouth without tilting it to the side." I carefully removed a cigarette holding it perfectly horizontal and placed it in my mouth and lit it, inhaled and said, *"This thing tastes like camel shit, but what the hell do you want for 90 cents a case."*

Groucho seemed please that he got a bargain and hoarded off his treasure to his locker.

Rape of the Cargo Handlers

In a few days, we were going to be redeployed to the South Pole, the bottom of the whole world, some of the men were getting restless, and some were just mean. One night we were playing cards when Mario and Luigi left along with some others. I did not have a good feeling about it and I was hoping they were not going to get into some trouble. They were gone about 45 minutes when all of the sudden they returned; bursting in the door laughing and in their hands they had 25-30 patches; one still had part of a shirt left to it. I said, *"OK what did you thugs do?"* Luigi said, "We went over to the cargo handler's quarters and we went in with our switchblades" and said, "Up against the walls--Mother Fuckers!" then we commenced to cutting these patches off their shirts. The pussies did not even try to resist-We were hoping for a fight. I mean the damn coasties didn't come in this year and we needed some souvenirs and action."

I was just at a loss that anyone would do such a thing for fun. I guess I was naïve.

Preparations for the South Pole

The rest of the week was uneventful and we were working hard. The others and I had been working in supply, unloading tools and equipment needed at the South Pole. The supplies were stored in the top floor of a building and were let down through a hole in the floor. The pallets of supplies were then lowered through it by block and tackle system. The job was very time consuming, not because it was hard work, but because the building was heated so we kept the job going as long as possible.

During the whole day, Groucho was trying to give to the others and me one of his packs of "Chesterfields" but no one would take a pack of his camel shit cigarettes and he started to get on our nerves.

Later that night when we were all in our beds, many of the guys were not tired; so we sat up late talking. Groucho, however, was dejected because of the shit people had given him all day over his cigarettes and was trying to sleep. Finally, he got angry and shouted out, "Hey, why don't you guys shut the hell up and go to sleep". Of course, that caused a maelstrom. All the sudden it started, "Roman"—ooooohhhhhh, "Rooomaaaan" "does Groucho need his sleepy." Then the guys started running over and shaking him in his mummy sleeping bag. I was afraid Groucho would lose it and due to his size, somebody would get hurt.

I decided to intervene, *"OK OK you guy's knock it off! Groucho let me ask you one question, Are you all zipped up in your sleeping bag nice and warm."* Groucho responded angrily "Yes, now shut the lights off and leave me alone."

I then gave hand signals to the men to quietly sneak over to Groucho's rack. Slowly and quietly, we moved over to Groucho zipped in his sleeping bag. He was on a top rack; when we all got there, I gave the signal and we pounced. Suddenly a dozen hands were on Groucho's sleeping bag. We lifted him up. God, he was heavy and we started carrying partly dragging him in his bag to the back door. Somehow, he managed to get his hands out the bag just as we were carrying him through the entryway outside and the struggle began in earnest; who would think one guy could almost overpower six others. Eventually we won; well we got him outside anyway, halfway out his bag and all of us naked in the snow freezing. After the laughter subsided, we all went back in and it was lights out.

The next day we were not as fortunate and we were instructed to train on constructing Wonder Arch out in the cold.

"The Wonder Building™ utilizes the strongest shape known in construction - an arch - not only in its silhouette but also in each panel. This means it can support great loads without even one internal support! No trusses, no frames, no support posts, and no purlins - just strong, sheet steel panels." (http://wonderbuilding.com/wb_history.html, 2006)

As we were working, I started climbing up the side of the 22 foot arch using a rope when all of the sudden the rope went lose and I was falling, and then all of the sudden my fall was abated. When I got to the top, there was Brillo. He had seen the rope loosen from its mooring and quickly grabbed it, partly burning his hands. Thanks to him, I was not injured.

November 9th--Tobacco Throwers War

The next night we were all getting ready to leave, it was our last night in the hut in McMurdo. In a few hours, we would be loading the plane for the South Pole. We had already turned in our baggage, bed linens and clothes except for the clothes we had on and our survival gear and then we got the word we were not leaving until the morning.

We were all so bored just waiting when someone turned out the lights the next thing I knew somebody attacked me from the top of one of the lockers. It was a bar fight in the dark! I tried to pull my attacker down and accidently closed the locker door on his thumb breaking it. We turned the Lights on.

We start to settle down when Groucho was still trying to get rid of the case of the Chesterfields. He threw a pack at me and hit me in the forehead. I got mad and threw it back at him and then him back at me and so on. Finally, I ran up, grabbed a carton of the Chesterfields, and started throwing them in rapid succession at Groucho then the others. Then Brillo, Mountain, Hoombag and the others ran over and started grabbing cartons and packs started going everywhere.

We then broke into teams, quite by accident, we just rather moved into groups. The group I was with got the "short end of the stick" in the war, Groucho and the others had most of the Chesterfield packs. We continued firing but we soon ran out of supplies. The "Shells" were flying and we had to retreat into the kitchen, but we were not going to surrender, we took turns jumping in front of the doorway and dodging the "bullets" while the others collected them for one gallant charge. I yelled, *"Forward men!"* The fighting was fierce. I started pelleting Hoombag and he then jumped on his bed and hid behind his survival pants and used them

"SW3 Hoombag Snag-a-dagg Bragg" *he moved*

as a shield and would stick his face out, and then stick his tongue out in a teasing way.

Finally, we drove them back and most of them out the door into the cold. Both sides suffered heavy casualties, but the biggest casualty was the hut. The fighting subsided and small flakes of tobacco where floating in the air. There was peace at last and all about us was the stench of war and its residue.

I then decided to rest and had my back to the door the next thing I knew there was Mario attacking me from the back and started to spray water from the fire extinguisher in my eyes. Instantly I was blinded because the water had antifreeze in it to keep it from freezing. I could not see and I was helpless and the pain in my eyes was immense. It was then that Mario puts his arm around my neck and whispered, "This is payback for threating to turn us in." I was in extreme pain when suddenly someone grabbed me and dragged me outside; blindly I had no choice but to follow. Finally, I was dragged into the shower, roughly stripped of my clothing while being struck and someone holds my head and eyes in the shower to remove the antifreeze. Afterwards I was dragged back to the hut and dumped in a rack. I was angry and saddened. I now realized that I was being persecuted in a small way for my faith. When I woke everyone else was asleep. I noticed they also trashed the place, I was angry and thinking of revenge but then I heard in my head "turn the other cheek." I decide to put the revenge out of my mind, swallow what little pride I had and cleaned up their mess as a gesture of good for evil to "turn the other cheek." I would never mention it again nor would I seek revenge deciding to leave the matter to God who knows all men's hearts.

Destination 90 Degrees South with Broke Dick Airlines

We mustered for the 14th time to go to the South Pole. We got all the way to the plane this time before it was canceled.

Finally, on the morning of November 12th at 5 a.m. we took off for the pole. We loaded a C130 Hercules propeller driven cargo plane especially equipped with skis on the wheels for the take-off and landing on the Pole. The flight time was three hours. We entered the plane with the propellers turning, because of the extreme cold, the pilots did not totally shut down the engines or else they would had soon froze or seized up. After the cargo was loaded, we shuffle into the belly of the beast. The seats were simple affairs of fold down web seats. I end up sitting right next to a window with a view of the propellers for a noisy flight. We affectionately refer to the people who fly and operate the planes between McMurdo and the South Pole as "Broke Dick Airlines."

As we're flying I noticed there was a red safety line running on the floor of the plane just to the right of me. Then I noticed there was a second red line running parallel with it and they were about two feet apart. The double redlines run along the entire inside of the plane cutting the plane in half and I wondered what their purpose was? During the flight, I enjoyed myself as best I could at 50 below zero and I thought of the first time I was in snow and my mind went back to Davisville during "A" School.

Midnight raid on the midrats—Davisville R.I.

Midrats are dinner leftovers served around midnight to those coming off the 2000-2400 watch and to those going on the 0000-0400 (balls to four) watch onboard U.S. Naval Vessels. (Anon., 1999-2011) We were not aboard ship but most things in the Navy ran as if we were.

It was late almost midnight and I was studying in my bed by a small lamp for our exams when Wolfman jumps out of bed in his underwear and puts on his watch cap and then pulls shoe polish out of his locker and starts to rub it on his face. I thought he must be sleep walking I got out of bed and shake him-he was awake.

I say, *"What, the hell are you doing Wolfman?"* He said, "I am starving and I am going down to the quarterdeck and steal me some midrats to eat."

I was hungry too and thought this might be some fun so I grabbed my watch cap too. The game was on. The plan was simple, taking a double razor with us, in nothing but our white underwear and watch caps. Silently, we left the room and entered the laundry room adjacent to our room. We opened the window crawled out on the snow covered overhanging ledge and with razor blade in our teeth; we did a commando style jump to the ground below. Our intent was to crawl in the snow take the razorblade out of our teeth slit the plastic bag hanging out the quarterdeck window and run off with the midrats and yes the plan worked perfectly but it was hardly worth the horsecock sandwiches we consumed.

Just then the Crew Chief of the C130 comes by and tells us we were landing and to buckle up. I was curious and I had to ask him about the red lines. *"Hey, what are the red lines for?"* He replied that we were to stay out from between those red lines at all costs. I said, "Why?" to which he states, "Well in a crash landing the propeller might come off and when it does it will cut through the plane right between those red lines" Holy shit, just my luck to sit here but then I consoled myself with the thought that really never happens. Just then, we feel the plane coming down and start to slide as it hits the frozen runway. I felt a sense of relief that we landed

safely and thought he was lying that shit never happens. As I thought about this, I looked out the window and I saw a crashed C130 adjacent to the runway. I was told it crashed the year before and yes, the propeller did cut it in half—Gulp!

November 12th the Old South Pole

When we arrived we were taken to the old South Pole it was underground and had at least 20 feet of snow over the top of it and we were led down; it was dimly lit, and it was like being in a mine. We were led into the Galley where we were served a hot meal. Man I was hungry all the sudden. I was hoping we were not getting horsecock sandwiches. As I take my tray of food over to the booth to eat I notice that this was the most unusual Galley I have ever been in. There under the glass of the table were playboy pinups. It was just a reminder for the men of the opposite sex for in 1973 women[4] were not allowed in Mobile Construction Battalions or at the South Pole. After we finished eating, and believe me some guys took a long time, we were shuffled out through the maze of tunnels. We walked on pallets past a small park the old poler's had built in the tunnel way. It had a small patch of artificial grass with a white picket fence around it with a sign that said, "Keep off the Grass"

---

[4] In 1972 women were granted entry into all Navy ranks by then Admiral Elmo Zumwalt, but it wasn't until 1994 that women were permitted to be assigned in Mobile Construction Battalions. In November 2011, Eight Seabee women from MCB 4 formed the first all-female construction team building two B-Huts at a Special Operations Base in Helmand Province Afghanistan.

6 DRY GULCH, ANTARCTICA

Finally, we arrived at our construction quarters. The year before MCB71 stayed at the old pole while they constructed our living quarters in a town they called Dry Gulch. Everything in it had a western theme. Hell we even had a Saloon—the **"Last Chance Saloon."** In typical western saloon fashion, it had liquor in the front and poker in the back.

We loved our commander LCDR Bill Kay because he knew and understood us. The following quote was obtained from www.southpolestation.com :

> "As a diversion from their incredibly difficult workload, I let the men construct a recreation room from shipping crates. Their typical Seabee cleverness and talent eventually resulted in the Hollywood type facade for the Last Chance Saloon, complete with hitching post (honest!). Another well-known trait of Seabees is their absolutely uncanny ability to create things from thin air, and the appearance of that shuffleboard, pool table and foosball game still bewilder me to this day!"
> (LCDR Kay CO of MCB-71)

Also the following article was from the Ice Cap News, May-June 1974. This journal was published by the American Society of Polar Philatelists (ASPP).

1973-74 U. S. ANTARCTIC RESEARCH PROGRAM OPERATION DEEP FREEZE AND NSF PHOTOGRAPHS

1. Dry Gulch City, South Pole, Antarctica. Welcome to the last frontier -- "Dry Gulch City"-- where it's always cold and the air is dry because we're at just over 10,000 feet altitude at the bottom of the world. Lt-Cdr Richard Carlson, from Butler, N. J., is the mayor of Dry Gulch, which had an average population of some 120 Seabees of Mobile Construction Battalion 71 in its eight buildings. When one ventures around the city you see such rustic sights as the famous "Last Chance Saloon" where the Seabees spend a lot of their off time; the "Court House," or headquarters building where the city's paperwork is done; and surrounding sites. If the men don't go to the movies, then they are likely to head for the "Last Chance Saloon" where there is always excitement. Sundays are a day of relaxation for most of the Seabees. However, there are a select few whose talents are needed: the chef and his staff work with dedication, and of course the bartender is on duty at the Saloon when it's open after work. Towards the end of this deployment in Feb. (1974), "Dry Gulch" will be a ghost town as the MCB-71 Seabees return to Davisville, Rhode Island. It will be the end of a town constructed to withstand snow, 100 mile per hour winds and temperatures of minus 80° and lower, but there will be left in its place a new station for U. S. scientists who will continue to probe for science at the bottom of the world. The good and the tough times at Dry Gulch City will be only memories to the Seabees

with MCB-71 after this season and will certainly provide a number of "sea stories" for many years to come.

2. Seabee Ingenuity. Looking more **like** Miss Kitty's Longbranch Saloon in Dodge, the Last Chance Saloon in Dry Gulch, Antarctica is the favorite place of the Navy men serving in support of science on the Great White Continent. It is designed and built by the men of Mobile Construction Battalion 71 from scrap materials, old packing crates, or anything else they could find. Everything is handmade, including the furniture.

3. Welcome to Dry Gulch. The city limits sign, normal with any small village or township, is found on the edge of Dry Gulch, Antarctica. The population of 146 represents the construction personnel of MCB-71 who built the new geodesic dome as the new station at the South Pole

4. Home at the end of a long day. Members of MCB-71 trudge **through** the main (and only) street in Dry Gulch. This construction camp is the home of these Navy Seabees during the austral summer during their deployment to the South Pole at the Bottom of the World. (Anon., n.d.)

All of the Jamesways in Dry Gulch had western names. The entire Steelworker clan and I ended up in the **"Dry Gulch Morgue"** they planted me on one of the top racks.

The front entry way was how we got in and out. In the back entry way a hole was cut in the material to which a large tin funnel was inserted. On the outside, a hose was attached and placed in a 55-gallon drum. This was a real convenience, now when you had to take a piss you could just run to the entryway open the door, piss in the funnel; be done, no wind, and not feel the cold before you were back inside the hut. However, there was one very important safety tip. DO NOT ALLOW YOUR DICK TO TOUCH THE FUNNEL! One Alfred Schlagel came in drunk and did so. Yes, his member froze to the funnel and all of the sudden, I heard awful screaming coming from the vestibule. Several others and I ran over to witness the tragedy. I must admit it was very amusing. Several of our experienced ICEMEN were not worried and knew exactly what to do. I thought Alfred knew too, from the fear in his eyes. With Zippos in hand they heated the metal of the funnel along with other tender parts and maybe even a few hairs until the funnel slowly released its hold on Alfred's penis and of course his dignity was wounded more than his fond member. I was sure the next time he approached the piss station he did so with more caution. It was also interesting to note that the 55-gallon drum filled before the end of the deployment. A few days before we departed the South Pole in February I went out there and we had formed a 10-foot wide 30-40 foot long 6-inch deep piss glacier from the overflow on the 55-gallon drum. I could not believe we pissed that much.

As far as our other necessary's went we had the same crapper configuration as at McMurdo, however, here there was no stink. That was great—the main reason was the crap froze as soon as it hit the can. Our shower facility also had showers and sinks. We were restricted to showering once a week, because every bit of water we used must be made from melted snow and it takes a ton of snow to make a little water. My hope was that they did not use any of that yellow snow! We also had a galley with our own cooks. We did not have fresh vegetables or eggs and such. Powdered eggs sucked but when you were hungry, you ate them. We had steak and lobster but it was funny the steak tasted like fish—I was told that was because the cattle were fed fishmeal.

South Pole Construction

Going out to the construction site for the first time we dressed warm. Almost immediately, I found out that it was really much colder at the Pole then it was at McMurdo. I was not ready for the difference and on the first day working; I almost got frostbit twice. I found out that due to my bowed long legs the bunny boots were cutting into the outer part of my legs and I needed to get issued to me Air Force Artic Mukluks these were "cold weather boots designed for use in dry cold conditions down to zero degrees F. The components of this system include 2 wool felt sole pads, 1 heavy wool bootie in each tall zip-up canvas outer shell to seal in the warmth, but not waterproof-dry cold only. Mukluks were designed to fit loose to allow for proper blood circulation, which was the key ingredient to keeping your feet warm." *(Anon., 2012)* I tried to wear the many-pockets pants but found I could hardly move in them so I only wore my long johns and uniform pants on my legs and was able to work without them. It was interesting to note that years later I had a body fat analysis done and it was discovered that I have a higher than normal fat to muscle make up in my legs.

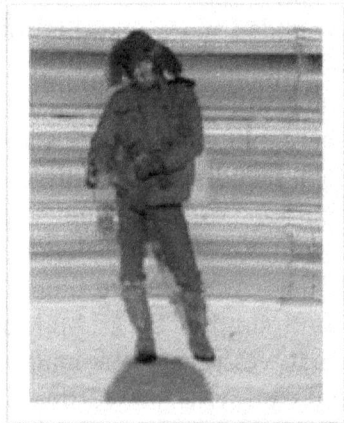

I wonder if my body actually deposited fat there to protect my legs. In regards to that thought, we also notice that most people's faces were getting fatter looking the longer you were at the pole.

I was so thin that the air would shoot right up my field jacket and the cold froze the shit out of me. I solved that problem by taking my wool scarf off, tying it around my waist tightly, and wearing a balaclava instead.

My hands were always exposed I tried to wear the bearclaws but could not move my fingers and I needed great manual dexterity in constructing the wonder arch. I just worked fast to keep my hands from freezing. I just draped the bearclaws by the connection strap around my shoulders and used the soft fur to wipe my nose, which was constantly running. After a short time my nose had gotten so raw that I could not even bare to touch it with the fur. Instead, and this was kind of gross, I just let the snot run until it formed a 12 inch "snoticicle" and then I would just break it off. I wore on my right "hammer" hand one military green wool glove with a leather mitten and on my left hand; I wore two pair of green wool gloves. I didn't wear a mitten on the left hand because I needed the dexterity to handle inserting the bolts in the wonder arch and used the two marlin spikes to align the arches precut holes.

As you can see from this drawing, we were working on the outer protective shell of the South Pole Station.

The first few days we finished some work on the dome. The dome was an engineering wonder that was as high as a five-story building. It was made up of triangular struts covered by sheet metal.

It had enormous strength and stability. Inside the dome, our builders were constructing three buildings on stilts to keep transfer of heat to the snow at a minimum. This was one of the reasons we were constructing this station. The footings for the dome and the wonder arch must be done properly. If the footing failed, the project could collapse on itself. Care was taken to ensure the footings were as solid as possible. To do this we used a specially designed machine from Switzerland, which actually dug a trench and then melted the snow depositing a firm ICE footing for the structures to rest upon.

The Steelworker crew and I were assigned to putting wonder arch sections together. We put together a row of the sections of various sizes of wonder arch in a preset pattern. The arch was connected using Huck® bolts. The three rows of arch once connected

"Danks" nose warmer on face

was about Seven foot high. After we had completed a three-row section it was lifted by Crane onto the footing and then the section was bolted together using standard bolt and nuts to construct the outer shell protecting the buildings inside the arch. It was a slow and lengthy process. The Huck bolt was designed like a rivet. I had to put the bolt in place and I used marlin spikes to align the wonder arch with the predrilled holes. Then once the hole was aligned

LockBolt Installation Sequence

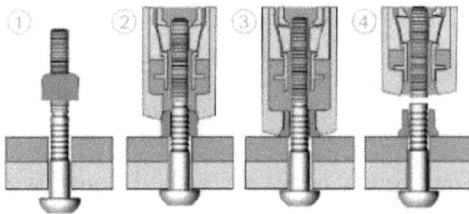

Huck bolt and collar

enough to slip the end of the bolt in the hole I would drive it home using a 12-pound sledgehammer. Danks, my partner would slip on a

Huck bolt collar put the hydraulic gun over the collar. The gun then crimped it, broke off the excess bolt, and shot it out the back of the gun. I have inserted the Huck Bolt technical drawings by the manufacturer Alcoa. (Anon., 2010)

Danks and I worked as a team. It was hard to breathe and we got tired by just walking because of the temperature and because we were sitting on 10,000 feet of ice, and the air was thin.

At the end of the day's work, which was normally 11 hours, we trudge ourselves back to the morgue then to the galley for a meal and maybe a drink at the saloon; then we would hit the rack.

The days seemed to blur together it was work, work, work. Some days were warm -17 and some days were cold -79.

In the early days, we would go outside worked like hell for 20 minutes and then would come into the warm up hut for 2 hours. We knew that shit was not going to last for too long so we milked it as long as we could. Then one day Steelworker Chief Sunshine, we called him that because he was bald, came in and angrily kicked us out saying. "Don't come back in until I tell you." Jesus! Two hours later frozen stiff barely able to walk he invited us back in. Now the cycle reversed-20 minutes in the hut/two hours of working as fast as you could to keep warm. As Steelworkers, we suffered as we were outside all season.

At night, everyone suffered from thirst due to the dryness. I would have to get up 2 or 3 times a night to slack my thirst and then found myself tired in the morning. I slept on the top rack (*toward the end of the deployment a lower rack became available—I slept in it one night –froze my ass off; as luck would have it*) and because hot air rises I would sweat at night and then froze in the morning.

It was like being in purgatory, as described by a pious man by the name Drithelm, who had a near death experience, in Fr. F. X. Shouppe's book "Purgatory".

> "On leaving my body, I was received by a benevolent person, who took me under his guidance. His face was brilliant, and he appeared surrounded with light. He arrived at a large deep valley of immense extent, all fire on one side, all ice and snow on the other; on the one hand braziers and caldrons of flame, on the other the most intense cold and the blast of a glacial

wind." "This mysterious valley was filled with innumerable souls, which, tossed as by a furious tempest, threw themselves from one side to the other. When they could no longer endure the violence of the fire, they sought relief amidst the ice and snow; but finding only a new torture, they cast themselves again into the midst of the flames." (Fr. F. X. Shouppe, 1973)

16 November-The Fun Continues

Every morning we were woken up by Petty Officer First Class "Pain in the ASS", he was screaming at us to get up, drop our cocks, and grab our socks. Every morning he said the same thing, **"Alright gentlemen get up—remember it is not the monetary value but the honor, privilege and glory to serve."** Rumor had it that "waking us up" was "Pain in the Asses" only duty. All we knew was he was never at the jobsite. It was also rumored that he drank a fifth daily, I refused to believe that. It was probably half a fifth.

At night while sweating, I prayed that the next day I would not be as cold tomorrow as I was today. It did seem to be working as I was up to almost 90 minutes of relative comfort before I needed to warm up. On my forearms, there were cold burns from where my coat and gloves separated as my arms were 2-3 inches longer than my jacket.

It was funny now that I am now nearly 60 years old and there have appeared on my arms half-inch age spots on the exact same place my coat and gloves separated on both of my arms.

7 THE BLUE RIBBON OF PAIN

19 November-Last Chance Saloon

After work, a friend of mine got sick while tending the bar so I took over for him. Drinking was an art at the Pole and there was more than one Dutch master. I made a lot of Dino specials. Dino specials were five shots of "Wild Turkey" with one shot of Coke. I did not know that a person could have drank that much and still lived. As a bartender, I did not have to worry about money. The bar used a club card with punches for drinks; Seabees only needed to sign for a card and at the end of the deployment the money was deducted before their pay. I was sure some had a much smaller end of deployment check than others did. The card cost $5.00 for twenty drinks and cigarettes were 15 cents a pack. I know that does not sound like too much but a 1973 dollar would be worth $5.00 in 2012. Therefore, a beer cost $1.25 at the Last Chance Saloon in today's dollars.

That night while I was tending bar Mountain jumped over the bar and then picked me up like a baby. He then put me over the bar and all the crew took me outside, proceeded to strip me of all my clothing, and buried me up to my neck in snow. It was official I was now a full member of the Emperor Penguins Court, South Pole Detachment and I had a blue ribbon on my uniform to prove it.

For the rest of that evening I tended bar in my underwear, as my clothes were drying.

After all that fun, I thought I really needed a day off. I was happy to hear that on Sundays we were going to be given a half a day off. I also heard we were going to get a whole day off for Thanksgiving. Maybe my prayers were working!

Military Amateur Radio Station (MARS) Phone Patches

Although the pain from the frigid weather was excruciating a lot of the men experienced a far greater pain because they dearly missed their loved ones. This pain was agonizing for most.

While I was on the ICE a thought entered my head that we had conditions worse there than most prison inmates. I thought, we worked 11 hours a day; how long do prisoners work? We did not get letters often from home; prisoners almost daily. We showered once a week; prisoners almost daily. We did not get phone calls from home; prisoners almost daily.

However, we did have the MARS station and a thing they called a phone patch. Back in 1974, we did not have internet, cellphones; microwaves or any of the electronic toys. Hell, Pac Man was not even around until the 1980's. We were utterly alone and isolated.

This was where MARS came in. MARS was a Ham radio station with a phone attached you talked into the phone just like normal but because it was radio, you had to say "over". The operator searched for another station on

KC4USZ
90° South
SEABEE BATTALION 7?

the radio to patch a phone call through and then you could talk to someone from home.

On Sunday, it was my chance to make a phone patch to my parents everything worked great but then I found out they changed their number. What! Here I was in Antarctica working my ass off; freezing my ass off and my alcoholic Father changed the phone number and too make matters worse I knew nothing of what was going on with my parents because they hadn't written me in the two years I had been in the Navy. I thought, "That's it, I am an orphan."

After my failed phone patch, I went to Mass. The Catholic Priest from McMurdo took a flight up to bring us Holy Communion. We had not been able to receive Communion since we left. I felt good after receiving Our Lord. I thought that even though I had no communication with my physical Father I did have communication with my eternal Father. Afterwards I showed the Priest around the site, before he left he said that he had a letter from the Bishop which gave me permission (Back then only Priests could give communion) to secure and give Holy Communion to the Catholic Boys there at the South Pole. I didn't feel worthy; come on this is Richard you know; but the Priest convinced me that it was the only way and I did want to bring "Our Lord" to my fellow brothers in Christ.

I thought about my experiences in Barbados, West Indies where I had a friendly relationship with a Jesuit Priest on the Island. I was stationed in Barbados after "A-School;" just prior to my assignment with MCB 71. It was luck or maybe providence that I got my first assignment to Barbados, West Indies. At the end of "A School", I ended up having the highest grade average-probably due to I studied and drank less than the others drank. The Chief had six orders for Vietnam and one set of orders for Barbados. I was given the orders to Barbados.

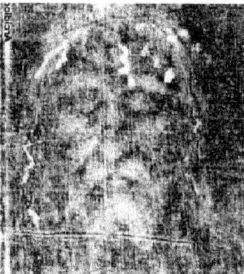

It was while I was in Barbados that I was examining my Catholic Faith and was considering a faith change because I was also involved with a non-Catholic Pentecostal religious group and because my Father had not practiced the Catholic Faith. I was at a point where I had to decide to be a Catholic or not. I was praying about it and one night I had a horrid dream where a horribly disfigured face appeared in white on a dark background. I woke up in a sweat.

I was disturbed by the thought of this vision. I got on my motorcycle and rode around the island. It was a four-hour ride. At the end of the ride, I passed a church and turned around to go in and pray. I knew I needed God in my life. After a short prayer, I was walking out of the church and there right next the exit door in a pamphlet rack, at eye level was the face in my dream. I was shocked, I pulled the pamphlet out and trembling read that this was the image of the reported face of Christ. It was on the burial cloth of Christ and was stored in a Catholic Church in Italy. I decided God was calling me back to the Catholic Faith. Why me? Why did he appear to me sinner that I was; I knew not. Yet, because of the memory of this call from Christ, I knew I had to consent to bring his precious body to my brother Seabees. The priest also left me a book to read. The book explained the Catholic faith. As I read it, I knew and understood my faith better. I was especially taken by an Old Catholic symbol and I drew it on a small red flag and wore that symbol on my back declaring myself an ICEMAN for Christ. The symbol means "Jesus Christ Conqueror" Now instead of a blue ribbon of pain. I had a flag for victory. I still was the same old sinner but the flag reminded me of God's ever presence; even here at the bottom of the world.

Work and Sleep

Almost all the Seabees at the Pole seemed to be getting a little irritable. All we did was work and sleep. The work was not that hard, the hardest thing was resisting the cold, as it was relentless; constantly draining your strength and essence. Mentally the work was no challenge; just rote. Grab steel put it together; align the holes with marlin spikes, place Huck bolt in hole; hit it with a BFH (big fucking hammer). Align the holes…you get the idea.
To break the monotony every once in a while you would get phlegm build up and we would spit it out on the wonder arch and watched it instantly freeze into a spit Rorschach.

The Rorschach inkblot test was a method of psychological evaluation. Psychologists use this test to try to examine the personality characteristics and emotional functioning of their patients. The Rorschach has been employed in diagnosing underlying thought disorder and differentiating psychotic from nonpsychotic thinking in cases where the patient was reluctant to openly admit to psychotic thinking. (Meloy, 1994)

Yes, we were psychotic and with your mind being so busy with this Rorschach stuff and such we started to notice things you didn't normally notice; like the sparling of the fine ice crystals always in the air; or the sound of your breathing, or even your own heartbeat thumping in your chest; or the comforting sound of the crunch of the snow under your feet, or the most amazing rainbow that forms completely around the sun when you looked up. Despite its hostile environment Antarctica was a place of unimaginable beauty.

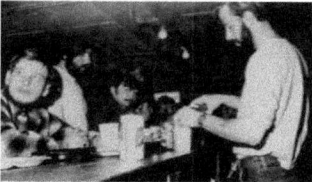

After work we all headed for the Last Chance Saloon. I didn't usually get intoxicated but people were giving me drinks left and right. So there I was in the center of the action with about 10-15 Seabees singing the "Old McDonald" song, however, this one had unique verses and gestures that went with it.

Old McDonald's Farm

Ol' MacDonald had a farm ee-eye-ee-eye-oh
And on this farm he had some chicks
With a chickee chickee here and a chickee chickee there
Here a Chick there a chick everywhere a chick chick

Ol' MacDonald had a farm ee-eye-ee-eye-oh
And on his farm he had a cow
With moo moo here and a moo moo there
Here a moo there a moo everywhere a moo moo

Ol' MacDonald had a farm ee-eye-ee-eye-oh
And on his farm he had a bull
With a bull bull here and a bull bull there
Here a bull there a bull everywhere a bull bull

Ol' MacDonald had a farm ee-eye-ee-eye-oh

And on his farm he had a cock…This was where the gestures came in—use your imagination. The last animal Ol' MacDonald had was a bear or should I say Bare.

After singing the night away, we kicked open the door to the Saloon and there burning holes in our drunken minds was the sun blaring, letting us know that in the Antarctic night the sun never sets. We headed back to the Morgue feeling pretty good but as Scarlet at the end of the "Gone with the Wind" novel says, "tomorrows another day".

The next day I was dragging it and as luck would have it, I was assigned to carry explosive gas materials that weighed 200 pounds; 50 pounds more than I did. Struggling, I finally got it to where it was to go without dropping it-then it was back to align the holes…

Thanksgiving

The evening of November 21st was a big party night—because by of a proclamation from President Nixon we were having the entire Thanksgiving Day off! The guys were excited. Some of the guys were planning to go over to the Old South Pole Station club but I was a little tired I thought I would just take it easy.

Proclamation 4255 - Thanksgiving Day, 1973

November 16, 1973

By the President of the United States of America

A Proclamation

In the first Thanksgiving, man affirmed his determination to live in God's grace and to act in God's will on the shores of a new land of promise. In this Thanksgiving season we reaffirm that determination.

Time has not dimmed, not circumstance diminished the need for God's hand in all that America may justly endeavor. In times of trial and of triumph that single truth reasserts itself, and a people who have never bowed before men go gladly to their knees in submission to divine power, and in thanks for divine sustenance.

On this Thanksgiving Day we mark the 10th anniversary of the tragic death of President John F. Kennedy. As we give thanks for the bounty and goodness of our land, therefore, let us also pause to reflect on President Kennedy's contributions to the life of this Nation we love so dearly.

Those who celebrated the first thanksgiving had endured hardship and loss, but they kept alive their hope and their faith. Throughout our history, each generation has endured hardship and loss, but our faith and trust in God's providence has remained undiminished. At this first thanksgiving in twelve years in which the United States will have been at peace, we see that God's grace also remain undiminished. For this we give thanks.

Now, Therefore, I, Richard M. Nixon, President of the United States of America, in accordance with the wish of the Congress as expressed in Section 6103 of Title 5 of the United States Code, do hereby proclaim Thursday, November 22, 1973, as a day of national thanksgiving, and concurrently, a day of prayer for the memory of John F. Kennedy. Let all Americans unite on this day, giving thanks for the manifold blessings vouchsafed our people, and inviting all of those less fortunate than ourselves to share in those blessings in God's name, for His sake, and for our own.

In Witness Whereof, I have hereunto set my hand this sixteenth day of November, in the year of our Lord nineteen hundred seventy-three, and of the Independence of the United States of America the one hundred ninety-eighth. RICHARD NIXON

Old Blue Balls

Most of the guys had a big night at the club. As I said, I was tired and did not go with the guys to the old pole station. In retrospect, I now wish I had; as I was told that it was really a good night. A couple of guys stole one of the dozers and went for a joy ride apparently they were riding around at the old pole and crashed through the roof into one of the buildings. Another group took Petty Officer First Class "Pain in the ASS" over to the old pole bar and started to buy him drinks all night. As the story goes, they kept libating him until he passed out and then convinced the medical officer at the Old South Pole to don his rubber gloves and paint his balls with blue indigo ink. Now, I do not know about you but that indigo ink was the same ink they put in Levi jeans. I heard tell that the Levi jeans company still has a pair of jeans from the 1800's that are still blue. I will bet Ol' blue balls'--balls are still blue!

Club 250

Brillo and I decided to use the day off to head on over to the South Pole ourselves. It was about a half a mile away but it took us a lot longer than we thought. It was slow trekking the distance through the loose snow. Along the way, we passed a railroad sign that some humorous person put up out there. When we got there, our intent was to get in the sauna, which was about 200 degrees. We stripped and got in. It was about the first time I had felt warm the whole time I had been there.

While we were in the sauna we decided today was the day we were going to join club 250. As soon as we got so warm we couldn't stand it anymore; we jumped out of the sauna nothing but our boots running the distance from the sauna; up a 100 foot ramp to the outside of the station where it was about 50 below zero. Thus the name, club 250, we went from plus 200 to minus 50 and made a 250 degree temperature change.

We ran over to the international marker for the South Pole with signs to all the different places and flags from many nations. It was interesting because even though Brillo was right next to me all I saw was a cloud because his body was giving off so much steam. When we got to the international marker, we ran around the pole three times and then headed back to the sauna. I mean think about it we just ran around the world naked three times. "Can you dig it" (70's slang for Do you understand?)

Brillo and I quickly headed back to the sauna as we were just beginning to lose our steam.

After we had, had a good warm up, we headed back on up to the international marker this time with our clothes on, too take pictures. Brillo mentioned that the other day a guy brought his golf balls and club over here and putted around the world in two strokes. I said, O' that's nothing and started to relieve myself with my back to the pole making a 360 degree turn and whizzed around the world.

After we got back to camp, we ate our Thanksgiving meal, watched movies, and of course stopped off at the Last Chance Saloon.

Hi Ho Hi Ho, It's Off To Work We Go!!

November 23rd. Ol' blue balls said again, as he did every morning, "Alright gentlemen get up—remember it is not the monetary value but the honor, privilege and glory to serve." Then it was grab steel put it together; align the holes with marlin spikes, place Huck bolt in hole; hit it with a BFH…

We needed to make up for lost time and as a result we were outside for two and a half hours-talk about cold. When we came into the warm-up hut, our bodies started steaming like when you open the freezer door and the steam comes out. Nothing seemed to be going right; our wonder arch would not go together, then our portable generator quit and then our Huck unit quit. I guess the cold was getting to everything.

Yet, the one thing that was going right was we never ran out of hot chocolate. Every time we went in, we always had hot chocolate. It could have been the "chocolate fairy" that made sure the chocolate was there but I think it was Chief Sunshine. He took care of us; he even made a little sign with instructions on how to make hot chocolate from the powder without it getting all lumpy.

1. Put cacao in cup.
2. Pour tablespoon of water in and mix to a muddy consistency.
3. Fill halfway stir.
4. Fill all the way stir.
5. Enjoy.

Every time we came in, we would throw our frozen cold wet gloves directly on the stove to heat them up and keep our hands warm. Occasionally someone would burn their gloves then they would shrink and stink something awful. After a while, I learned that I could extend my time outside by using the Huck engine exhaust to warm up the inside of my gloves.

The flu also seemed to be going around and everyone was coughing and had a sore throat. That night when we went home, we had a pleasant surprise; we got clean laundry and after wearing the same clothes for a month; it felt great to put on clean clothes.

After I ate I went straight to bed, I did not feel good. The next day I was on quarters. I had pulled a muscle in my back, I had strep throat and the frostbite on my arms was turning my arms brown. I later got longer long Johns and that seemed to take care of it.

November 30th. We did a lot of work putting the wonder arch together and after work we trudged on over to the airfield and took pictures of a C130 landing and pictures of the crashed airplane from the year before.

December 2nd. We ate fresh eggs for breakfast! We had not had fresh eggs since we got there and that night we had half a BBQ chicken, fries and a SALAD. We forgot how good this stuff tasted. Bless you Broke Dick Airlines!

December 3rd. Work was going great! The day was a balmy day only minus 20 degrees. After we finished work we headed on over to the Galley: It was Movie night. We saw "40 Pounds of Trouble" with Tony Curtis. It was a good movie but it was 11 years old. They spare no expense on our account. I wonder if the movie had been there since 1962. After the movie, I checked the seeds in a pan I planted in earth that my girl sent me. They were just starting to sprout. The earth was the closest dirt for 900 miles and those sprouts were the only plants that I knew of in Antarctica at the time. They were growing just from the lights in the room.

December 4th. It was a bad day to be out, it was cold minus 74 degrees; I think my boys froze.

December 5th. I saw my life flash before my eyes this day. I was not paying any attention and I inadvertently walked between the crane and the arch moving. If the operator had not been paying attention and stopped, I could have been cut in half. It was stupid of me, I was tired and I was not thinking. I was making it a habit at night to pray before I went to sleep. I was so tired all I got out was "God Bless these men" and I was out like a light.

December 6th. I was tired in the morning I did not want to get out of bed. Later that day, to make my disposition worse, I was a little upset with a junior steelworker whose assigned duties were to fill our Huck Riggs and portable generators with fuel from a 55 gallon drum using a hand fuel pump. We called this pump a hurdy gurdy because it had a small hand crank like the musical instrument of the same name. The pump had a metal pipe about three feet long that was inserted into the 55-gallon drum. The hurdy gurdy had a fuel hose, which was then put to the fuel tank to be filled, and the handle of the hurdy gurdy was turned to fill the fuel tank. I had to admit that being the hurdy gurdy man was not the best of jobs. You had to walk all over the job site constantly refueling equipment and your uniform got full of the fuel. I felt sorry for the guy and he didn't have the best attitude, go figure, and he left the hurdy gurdy in the hut and it leaked fuel all over the floor. Hoombag slipped on it when coming in. I told the hurdy gurdy man to clean it up but he refused. I was senior to him and I could have made an issue out of it but I did not and I just cleaned it up myself.

A few days later, he gave the same shitty attitude to the wrong people. They held him down, pulled his pants down and threaten to corn hole him and then started to rub Vaseline on his ass, and touched his ass with a hotdog. All this happened in the presence of the entire hut. I could not believe nobody tried to stop it. I was at the other end of the hut and started to walk over there to say something but then it was over as soon as it started. However, I must say the hurdy gurdy man had a marked improvement in his attitude after that.

December 7th. I worked inside, YES! It was the anniversary of the bombing of Pearl Harbor. It felt like Hawaii to me, compared to what I was used too. I was working on making an anti-pollution unit for the generators. The South Pole was pollution free, and they wanted to keep it that way.

We were having a crime spree in Antarctica. Last night someone tore up our shop. They threw paint all over, broke windows, and messed up our sheet metal ducting. Whoever it was, they were drinking and smoking pot. They sent the beer cans' in for fingerprints. I guess no place is safe from potheads; drunks or politicians.

That night I talked to the Protestant Chaplin about having a lay service for The Feast of the Immaculate Conception for the Catholics in camp. He gave permission to proceed and I put the word out.

December 8th. After work, I went over and set up to have a Lay Service for the Feast of the Immaculate Conception. I sat there by myself for an hour; none of the Catholics showed up? I was disappointed. The reason no one showed up was Groucho decided that he wanted to be like the winter over guys and cut all his hair off down to the bone but left his beard on. Eight people were standing around and watched him.

December 9th. I was sick this day I had what was called Alpine sickness it was from the high altitude, but I worked anyway. The Corpsman there gave you a hard time every time you went to see him, so I tried not to go to see him, unless I really needed too. I would cough a lot and it felt like I had a hole in my body where my lungs were. The Corpsman besides being our doctor was also our camp storekeeper. I went in there to buy some Christmas cards from him and I got into a coughing jag and the little caring prick said to me, "Where's my Oscar that was the most beautiful act I've ever seen." I was a little put off by that because this guy had no clue he never left the comfort of his store or medical office yet he ended up getting the same recognition as the Seabees at that place who suffered working outside every day.

After I got my Christmas cards I walked over to the old pole to take some pictures and I stopped by the bar there called Club 90. It was called that because the South Pole was 90 degrees south. After the beer I walked back; I had to lay down (not fall down) and stopped five times because of the Alpine sickness (not the alcohol) made it hard to walk.

December 10th. Some of the guys here have climbed up to the top of the Dome and slid down. I wanted to try it myself but no one would go with me and I was too chicken to do it by myself. One of our enlisted Seabees climbed up to the top and placed up there the State Flag of Pennsylvania. It takes a lot of courage to go up the dome; there was nothing to hold on to and if you slip, you could tear yourself apart on the bolts coming down.

We were instructed that reporters were coming to interview us and take pictures and due to politics Mr. Pennsylvania was instructed to go back up to the top of the dome and replace his flag with the US Flag, which he did.

We had formed a little solidarity in protest to this action because we did not like that politics, in a way, had nullified his courage to go up to the top of the dome. In the military, you could not really have a protest, yes, this was the 70's but this was the Navy. We all just rather agreed to act stupid for the reporters. I wore my top hat, Brillo wore his smoky the bear hat and we just generally acted stupid. One young man when asked how he liked it there said, "I love it here!" and started laughing hysterically. Do not get me wrong, we loved our US flag; what upset us was the way Mr. Pennsylvania's courage; was dishonored and used for some political

gain. "Things don't change much, do they?"

December 11th. When I got to the job site, I discovered they had changed my work assignment. I was to help with the bolting of the wonder arch sections together with the crane. I had to sit on the wonder arch to bolt it together. I asked Chief Sunshine if I could go back to the hut and get my many pockets pants on. I thought about what the cold steel did to our spit; you know the Rorschach inkblot test. I could not imagine what that steel would do to my ass. Unfortunately, the Chief said, "No." I literally froze my ass off. The next day I got up and my ass hurt something awful. I was not about to show my ass to Brillo so I had to go over to mister prick Corpsman. Yes, the cold burst the veins that surrounded my asshole. Holy Hemorrhoids and there was no preparation "H" in town. It brought back memories of my older sister who came home drunk one night and brushed her teeth with preparation "H." Pucker up baby! I was tired ass that evening so I went to bed early.

December 14th. I was on quarters this day. I had pulled my shoulder muscle; had strep throat along with the Alpine sickness and hemorrhoids. I slept all day and then I could not sleep that night.

December 15th. Back at work; it was grabbed steel put it together; aligned the holes with marlin spikes, placed Huck bolt in hole; hit it with a BFH. I was having difficulty getting the wonder arch to go together that day and I threw a temper tantrum. I took my frustrations out on the steel and started hitting it with my hammer and yelling. I felt better afterward. The shit was starting to get to me with the sickness and the cold along with lack of sleep and my ass hurt; I lost it.

Then I thought, come to think about it, many people around there were losing it. There was one young man there, who had it in his mind that he was going to wear his porkpie hat and not take it off until the end of deployment. The hat was really greasy and nasty and someone snatched it off his head and threw it down on the snow. Mr. Porkpie gave him a right hook, so hard, that it broke his jaw. He was medevac'd out of there.

We also had one Seabee quarantined in the tool crib. The tool crib was a small heated building halfway between the construction site and the camp. He was staying there because he had mononucleosis and he was contagious. He had probably had it for a while and it just appeared because this place had weakened his physical condition. Rumor had it that this guy was going to be medevac'd all the way back to Honolulu, Hawaii.

As we were working, I noticed a lot of the steelworker crews were disappearing. I found out that Luigi and Company had gone down to the tool crib with a fifth of whiskey and got drunk and started giving lip locks to Mr. Hawaii. In the end, nobody ended up going to Hawaii after all.

Pranks were starting to become more and more common. The other day some of the builders nailed BUCA Yak's boots to the floor. When he got up in the morning and he slipped his feet into his bunny boots, stood up, and tried to walk, he fell flat on his face. They tortured him because he was very outspoken about his religious ideologies and he went around telling everyone how they were going to burn in Hell. His accent was quite strong and his voice was a little irritating. He was from Arkansas. Yak's name was mud because he was upsetting many people. They pink bellied him and did other little tortures.

Chief Burnout decided that the men needed a little release with everyone having testosterone fever and he had nudie films played during the movie night. The evil pricks grabbed Yak and tied him in a seat when he would not come to the movie: he closed his eyes though. I was proud of his moral courage in face of this abuse. They just made more fun of him and said he was peeking.

Yak was not the only one tortured. Down at the other end of the morgue were Mario, Luigi and company. They attached a Pig's foot to the light string as a handle for the light. After a few days one of the guy's on that end of the Morgue got tired of it, pulled out his buck knife and cut the pigs foot off the string and threw it out the back door. While he was asleep Mario & Luigi went back out there and got the pigs foot attached it to another string. This time they suspended it two inches from his nose while he slept.

December 17th. I was finding it harder and harder to sleep at night—it was chronic insomnia. The old polies call it the Big Eye. It must have something to do with the sun being up all the time. I fell asleep around 3 a.m. The trick was to start praying until I fell asleep. I felt like total crappola in the morning and by the afternoon, it was worse. I could hardly pickup my hammer, but somehow, I made it through the day.

December 18th. My plant was growing and about 8 inches high and starting to flower. The cycle continued: We ate, slept and worked. As part of my morning, ritual on waking up I would immediately run out the back door to take a piss. There was nothing that could wake you up more in the morning then going from a room of plus 70 degrees to the outside with a temperature of minus 20 degrees. I was not the only one with this ritual; the Piss Glacier was growing as well as the plant.

December 20th. We finished the longest run of wonder arch 324 feet of arch. This section would hold fuel bladders to refuel the C130s. Everyone was excited, we were having a Christmas dance and you had to have a date to get into the dance. We drew lots; half the guys in camp were going to dress as women. I was hoping I could find a date for the dance. I was having a problem finding a date. What? Did my breath stink?

December 22nd. After work, we were all practicing playing football for the New Year's Day Pole Bowl game we were going to have. I was hoping to get a position and hoped to do well; so I could play in the Pole Bowl game. Some TV crews were in camp filming. They filmed Mr. Hurdy Gurdy and me walking over to the galley. I was a little embarrassed because he was jumping up and down giving them two peace signs.

My little plant was starting to wilt; I thought it probably needed sunlight. In an effort to save the plant I took out my buck knife and cut a hole in the Jamesway tent wall, about two inches long and I insert the cardboard from a roll of toilet paper to let sunlight in for my plant. An added benefit was that it was easier to sleep at night due to the fresh air coming in. Soon about five other guys suffering on the top bunks had little fresh air ports over their beds too.

8 CHRISTMAS DANCE AND BEYOND

December 24th. Well I did finally get a date for the dance. It was Lusty Lacy. Here is a picture of us. With my hand I an pulling up his dress to expose the girlie tatoo on his arm. One thing for sure was we were going to have a White Christmas.

We had a very nice Christmas Eve service with a Candle lighting ceremony lighting the four-advent candles. Each candle represents a wish for the world. The first was for *forgiveness;* the second was for *peace*; the third was for *joy* and the fourth was for *hope.*

A Southern Christmas
Article in the Transit (MCB 71 newspaper)
January 1974

"This season's Christmas festivities at the Pole began to materialize on Christmas Eve. We decided that we would work a full day on the Sunday before

Christmas so that we could have the afternoon of Christmas Eve off."

"The celebration began at noon with another of CS1 Goss' fine meals. The afternoon was spent by most either relaxing, playing cards and other games in our newly completed recreation building, or sleeping for those of us who got into the Christmas Spirits at the Last Chance Saloon the evening before. After supper Chaplain Roberts organized competitions in games such as darts, doubles pool, chess, ping pong, fusbol, cribbage, and pinochle."

"The Christmas Eve dance was the social highlight of the season. Guys and their dates began arriving at the Last Chance Saloon at about seven O'clock for early cocktails. The dance began at seven-thirty and lasted until eleven O'clock for those who were able to resist over indulging in the Christmas Spirits."

"The dates were lovely things, dressed in their best Christmas finery. The gowns salvaged from a Navy bundle proved quite colorful

and serviceable. Jim Bogati and Frank Saggio were definite standouts at the dance. However, the other lovelies were by no means wallflowers"

"Christmas Day was a beautiful, clear, windless day with the temperature reaching as high as minus 21 degrees. It was a perfect day for the Christmas football play-offs between the Charlie Company "Animals" and the Bravo Company, Holmes and Narver, and Alpha Company "Brutes" at the Richard E. Carlson Memorial Snow Field. Chaplain Roberts officiated the hot, tense, and emotional game and kept the action from erupting into uncontrolled violence as it often threatened to do. The game ended in a scoreless tie with the "Animals" attempting a feeble field goal with no long lasting injuries or grudges resulting."

"The game was followed by another of CS1 Goss' legendary, irresistibly delicious, holiday meals. He served up ham, steamship round, turkey, and dressing with all the trimmings. We all really enjoyed that meal. We would like to thank, also, the Wives Club for their thoughtfulness in sending us the scrumptious cookies and other delicacies." (Anon., 1974)

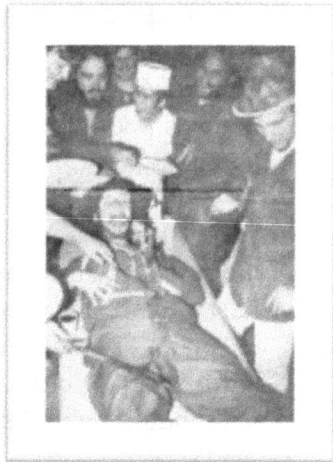

During the Christmas Dance I was tending bar when LCDR Bill Kay, our beloved commander came walking into the Saloon. He came all the way from McMurdo to spend time with us for Christmas. All of the sudden, I realized he had never been initiated into the Emperor Penguins Court, South Pole Detachment. We needed to rectify the situation immediately. I then made eye contact with Mountain and signal the surround the wagons signal to him. He got the message and grabbed Mr. Bill—Oh Nooooooo! I leapt over the bar and our crew of steelworkers moved in like a well oiled machine. We quickly escorted Mr. Bill outside the Saloon for the a royal initiation into the Emporor's Court and buried him naked, neck deep, in the ice. I immediately positioned myself six paces from the action and gave the command to *"Fall in"* The steelworker crew smartly fell into ranks.

I then did an about face and over my shoulder gave the command, *"Hand Salute"* we all gave our commander the proper hand salute and respect. On the way back into the Saloon I deposited the Blue Ribbon of Pain next to LCDR Kay's uniform as he dug his way outside of the snow.

The evening continued with singing, drinking and dancing. We sung the "Old McDonald Song" and another called "We like it here" and of course the "Seabee" song.

The Song of the Seabees

(1943)

Words by Sam M. Lewis Music by Peter de Rose

We're the Seabees of the Navy
we can build and we can fight
we'll pave the way to victory
and guard it day and night
and we promise that we remember
the "Seventh of December."
We're the Seabees of the Navy
Bees of the Seven Seas.
The Navy wanted men
That's where we came in
Mister Brown and Mister Jones
The Owens, the Cohens and Flynn
The Navy wanted more
Of Uncle Sammy's kin
So we all joined up
And brother we're in to win

Other festive activities included playing craps and of course there was a multitude of ass packings. One guy got his leg broke during an ass packing last week and since then he was assigned to be the duty laundry man. Mr. Laundry collected our dirty stuff and washed it; now we got clean underwear on nearly a weekly basis!

As crazy as it sounds I was thinking of putting in for a duty change to become a member of the Antartic Support Group and return there the next year.

Construction Continues

December 26th. Well, it was back to the salt mines after the Christmas festivities and before work I put the plant in the recreation center. It had large picture windows for more sunlight. After work, unfortunately I didn't know that the rec center was not heated when we were working and the plant froze. I ended up throwing it out back with the piss glacier.

December 29th. We finished constructing the arch for the power plant this day. So far we had completed the Dome, Fuel Bladders, Biomedical and power plant. All we had left to complete was the shop/recreation and helium storage areas. After work we were surprised with mail. It was the first mail we had received in 10 days.

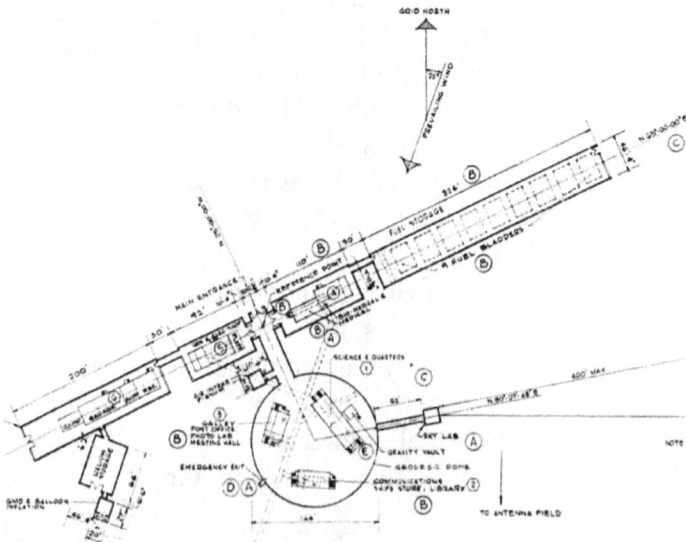

<u>December 31, 1973</u>. On the last day of that year, We closed it out by snow surfing. The arch that we were assembling was on top of a snowdrift, which was higher than where we were assembling it. As we grabbed the pieces, we noticed that they slid down the hill so we rode them down the hill for assembly. At one point Luigi, Mountain, Lacy and I all slid down on one piece of arch together. We smashed into some more arch and we went flying all over the place. At another point, we tried it standing up—snow surfer style. It was a beautiful day; I noticed that the reflection of the sun on the snow made it look like the sun was setting with a second sun—it was remarkable.

> "Thine, O Lord, was the greatness and the power and the glory and the victory and the majesty, indeed everything that was in the heavens and the earth; Thine was the dominion, O Lord, and Thou dost exalt Thyself." 1 Chronicles 29:11

Some of the crew was complaining that they were tired of the same job they had been doing. Therefore, I decided to talk to Chief and he asked them if they would like to switch jobs, they said no. I was perplexed because they made me look like an ass. I learned a valuable lesson that New Year's Eve: People just like to bitch. My New Year's resolution: *Do not take other people's problems on as your own.*

<u>January 2, 1974</u>. I was not feeling well but I worked anyway. We were trying to complete next year's work in one year so we would not have to return the next year. It was very cold in the afternoon and the wind was blowing hard. The wind would cut through you like a knife.

<u>January 6</u>th. Everything we got at the South Pole came in by Broke Dick Airlines, due to their efforts this day was a happy little Christmas; we got clean laundry and Schlitz' beer.

<u>January 10th</u>. We were getting close to the end; we were starting to clean up the job site. As we were picking up boards and stuff, I found a piece of plastic; which I used like it was a sled. I had the garbage track pull me to piles of trash as we picked them up. It was mindless entertainment combined with just pure laziness.

<u>January 11th</u>. This was the warmest day we had at the South Pole. It was minus six and there was not any wind; it was heaven. I was sweating and I was able to completely remove my jacket; then found that it was so warm I could also go shirtless for a while. I decided to get some sun and some needed vitamin D.

It occurred to me that day that even though we had snow on our clothes at all times that due to the extreme cold and dryness our clothes never did get wet from the snow.

<u>January 12th</u>. I was very busy during this time; working all day and studying at night. I was going up for promotion to Steelworker 2nd Class. I was to be tested on January 23rd there at the South Pole.

At work that day, we finished the last of the 44-foot arch and we started on the smaller connecting 21-foot arch that connects all the buildings.

On a personal note for this day: one of the other Petty Officers' from the Mario and Luigi side of the Morgue; challenged me to a fight because I didn't recommend his friend for promotion. I did not fight him nor did I recommend his deadbeat friend. I also resisted the temptation to say to him that if he wanted to fight;
"He could stick his head up my ass and fight for air."

<u>January 13th</u>. After work, I walked over to the plane crash from the year before. I took the co-pilots ditching (crash) instructions from the plane and the paratroopers light off it. It seemed like the boys from Broke Dick Airlines never used those instructions and were able to crash that plane without any instructions at all. I thought about putting the paratrooper light on my car when I get back to Davisville. Later that night I played poker at the Saloon and lost $11.00. Easy come easy go.

January 14th. We finished the last of the 21-foot arch. We had a few problems but they worked themselves out. We also started on the 9-foot arch that day. After work, two of my friends were fighting so I grabbed the both of them by their hair trying to stop them. That was a mistake. Both of them turned on me and grabbed me off my bed and they grabbed my pocket flap and tried to rip my trousers apart. I noticed a small hole in one of their trousers and stuck my finger in it and ripped the whole leg of his trousers off. It appeared I won the trousers ripping contest, with both of them walking off with their trousers in tatters. Mine were still intact.

January 16th. We were in the middle of the Antarctic summer. We were having a heat wave. The tent was sweltering at night. In desperation, I cut the hole bigger over my bed. The big eye was killing me and the heat in the room was making it worse. I was also becoming slovenly. I had not taken a shower in two weeks. I just did not want to shower and then crawl back into the same dirty clothes. In addition, we had not had a change of sheets on our beds in two months. We could almost stand the sheets up by themselves. Our caring ass corpsman came in and swabbed everyone's throats. Strep throat was going around. I suppose the heat inside was advancing the germs in the hut-it was becoming a real morgue.

January 17th. We finished the last Hucking of the wonder arch. The guys were starting to call me the Huck King because I took a Huck bolt put it through the top of my earflap hat. Looks like an old German World War I hat. I estimated that I had put in about 750,000 Huck bolts in the last two months. Boy was I happy. The next day Lacy and I would start working on the flanges for the arch; it would be a job a little more interesting.

I finally broke down and took a shower that night. I was trying to improve my slovenliness; I would be coming back to civilization soon and I needed to start cleaning up my habits.

<u>January 18th</u>. I made a bet with another steelworker. We were looking at the drawings for the entry way and I bet $100 on how we were supposed to apply the drawings. I was wrong. That was it no more betting. Maybe it was worth it in the way of wisdom. I thought, Alright, two more new rules *no betting* and *shower regularly*. Pretty soon I would be a regular altar boy.

<u>January 23rd</u>. I took my Petty Officer Second Class test this day. I thought I did not do very well, but then I thought time would tell. I was planning to getting married to my girl when we got back from deployment and the extra money would be a Godsend. Things were starting to slow down at the Pole. My hair was getting longer than it had ever been. I never was a long hair hippy type. My hair

was so long that I split my hair down the middle as the hippies do. I put a ribbon around my head and posed for a picture in front of the morgue.

I remembered the last time I parted my hair down the middle was back in Davisville. It was a lot shorter then and I was going to sheet metal layout school. As luck would have it, I was the last person in the galley for dinner and the head cook approached me and asked me if I wanted to go to a Don Rickle's Show in Providence. It seemed the Admiral could not use the ticket and gave it to the cook to give to a lucky Sailor or Seabee. Cool! Of course, I said yes. I parted my hair down the middle because I was going to a Don Rickle's Show and I wanted to be cool. What a mistake!

When I got to the coliseum, it was packed and unfortunately, I had a front row seat. There I was minding my own business laughing at the comedy routine when Don Rickle's caught sight of me and he started saying shit about me. Calling me a

Don Rickles

faggot and bringing me into the comedy show. Finally, he actually came down from the stage and asked me, "Hey faggot what is your name anyway." I was embarrassed and I thought quickly and came back with a good smart-ass answer. There was a popular country song back then so I said, *"My name is Sue; how do you do"* and the place roared. Don then turned to me and said, "Hey, faggot knock that shit off. I am the one being paid to do the comedy routines. You got a bigger laugh than I did!" and the place roared again.

January 27th. I had been trying to make a phone patch for the past couple of days to my girl but the radio reception was not good; they could not make a connection. That was unfortunate because the next day they were going to take down the antenna, as we were getting closer to leaving.

January 29th. The temperature was starting to drop again, it was a minus 56 degrees. We found out we were leaving February 7 and we were very excited. The change would be nice. I realized I had not seen stars since 13 October. I decided that on the first night I got back to New Zealand I would get a bottle of wine and watch the sunset. We were by that time taking turns sleeping in until 10 am because we were almost done there.

January 31st. It was a dry cold. Well that was what they said; so if it were zero there; it would feel like +25 in the States. You know I thought it was bullshit because if it was 80 below there it was still minus 55 in the States and that was still bloody colder than a witch's titty in a brass bra. In addition, it only snows one to two inches a year there at the pole; but the reason there was so much buildup of (four feet) snow each year was that the wind blows it there. I guess the wind has been blowing here for a while because there were 10, 000 feet of it there.

Legend of the Phantom Shitter

For about the last month there at the Pole, we had been experiencing a little problem. Someone had been shitting in the most peculiar places. The first time the *Phantom Shitter* deposited a big pile of his colon cannon balls or whatever you want to call it was in the tool crib. Then the Phantom next showed up depositing his creamy butt nuggets inside the cab of the crane. Toward the end when the builders were, working on the buildings in the Dome Mr. Phantom deposited another turd tunnel tasty right on Chief Burnout's desk. We thought that was uncalled for and then all the sudden the Phantom vanished. We did not know who he was and nobody would admit to it. To this day, I still do not know who the Phantom was. I do suspect that it was someone on the night crew.

The last day we were at the Pole, we were going to have a ribbon cutting ceremony with all of us in formation as our Commander was turning the station over to the National Science Foundation. In preparation for the ceremony, the night crew worked all night cleaning up the area. They needed to get fresh clean snow and spread six inches of it all over the jobsite because the snow at the jobsite was dirty and sooty from the engines, equipment and such. When we marched out there on that last day to our surprise the Phantom had struck.

There in the beautiful virgin white snow right next to the entrance to the new South Pole Station was the biggest ass squeezing I had ever seen. There next to, it was a stake with a roll of toilet paper and a sign, which read; "Here is your six inches of virgin snow," signed the *Phantom Shitter*.

South Pole Station at Dedication 1974

9 MCMURDO/CHEE CHEE AND A FORTNIGHT

We arrived back in McMurdo on 4 February ahead of schedule. I remember the first living thing I had seen was a bird. I had not seen a bird in the last three months. As we were driving from the ice runway into the McMurdo station we saw, about 100 dead seals piled up to feed the husky dogs of the New Zealand Army. I felt a little sorry for the seals but the dogs had to eat too. It was warm in McMurdo compared to the Pole. I was even surprised when I saw a small creek of water running; it shocked me because I thought that it would be too cold. It was so warm there +10 degrees. I was walking around in my T-shirt.

The air was a little heavy there too; we dropped two miles in altitude. When Brillo and I first got off the plane, it really felt weird; like we were missing something but we could not figure it out. Then all of the sudden I knew. I said, "Brillo, it's our breath; we can't see our breath." Yes, that was it. We thought it was funny how you get use to something and when it was missing, you do not somehow feel complete without it.

We fell right into life in McMurdo, soon we would be returning to CHEE-CHEE for two weeks of rest and recreation. After that, we would make the return trip back to Davisville. McMurdo was the same as it was before however, the crapper was even fouler. Now when you went in to take a crap; it was never frozen; stunk like hell and the cans were always full. I really hated it when you looked into each of the cans for the least full one and when you sat down you felt something soft hit your ass.

McMurdo was crowded and there were more people for the thugs to rough up at night. There were more fights than usual. The night of our return, someone broke into the Helium storage area and brought a bottle of helium to the club and all night long, we sang in Mickey Mouse voices because the Helium froze our vocal cords.

The next day we had a formal awards ceremony with the entire Battalion. We could not believe it when LCDR Kay called Brillo out of the formation and presented him with a medal, "The Purple Penis" Award for sacrifices made beyond the call of duty in support of Operation Deep Freeze. It was the biggest medal I had ever seen. There attached to a military purple ribbon was a life size metal purple penis. We were in McMurdo only a couple of days and then it was back to CHEE CHEE.

When we arrived back in CHEE CHEE it was great. It was probably cold there but to us it felt like Hawaii. We got to the barracks and I claimed a bottom rack. Soon Yak came in and claimed the rack above mine; I guess he felt safe with me and thought no one would mess with him above me. Yak went to the bathroom and I went over to talk to Brillo to see what he wanted to do. As I started back to the rack, Yak was walking in front of me, he got to the racks before me and jumped up on the top rack when all the sudden the whole mattress collapsed and Yak's rack came crashing down on my rack with Yak. Those evil pricks, I was pissed and started yelling, *"Hey that was my rack"* and the whole place was erupting in laughter. After I helped Yak fix his rack, Brillo and I were off on the town.

The first place we went was to a Tea Room. That was where I fell in love; with the first woman, I had seen since October. I was making an ass out of myself when Brillo grabbed me and we were off again—Jelly Bean time.

We had to endure another two weeks of muster and make it. It was hard to take. The time was a welcome relief from the rigors of Antarctica. I even learned to enjoy 4 o'clock teatime with milk in my tea.

I spent about three days during that time in New Zealand traveling the country and it was one of the most beautiful countries in the world. I almost got a Maori tattoo while I was there in Northern New Zealand. The Bees let off a lot of steam from the deployment during those two weeks. One night we were outside our barracks and there was an outside party. People were all over just enjoying the weather and of course there was alcohol being consumed when a couple of New Zealand girls showed up.

They were on the hunt and the hunting was plentiful. They were flirting with all the men. Then all the sudden someone I did not know walked out of the barracks with nothing but a Navy blanket wrapped around him and these two girls were trying to see what he had under the blanket. Well, he had the same thing a Scotsman has under his kilt. When all of the sudden these two girls started to attack him and almost engaged in a sexual Twix right there in the street with Mr. Blanket now laying down on his blanket; when I decided to intervene, and I said to the two New Zealand lovely's, *"Hey, girls how would you like a virgin?"* They stopped what they were doing and got excited and I immediately led them into the barracks where Yak was up on his rack reading. Immediately they attacked him and tried to disrobe him. I think he actually hit one of them and ran and locked himself in the bathroom.

I only meant it as a joke and I was trying to tell Yak I was sorry but every time I put my head up over the stall, he would try to hit me. I said I was sorry through the stall but by that time, the girls were back on the prowl again. People were running all over the barracks that night. I do not know when I fell asleep.

The next morning when I woke up people were out of control, one young man was throwing up and another was just coming out of a coma and said, "Have you ever woken up with the nasty taste of sex in your mouth and can't figure out which sex it was?" All I say was "Don't ask; don't tell! Finally, after two exhausting weeks, it was time to enter the C141 and make that 40-hour trip back to Davisville again.

I will never forget those days of glory and sacrifices we made; or the magnificence of the Antarctic continent. I can now heartily say along with my Seabee brothers that:

"The ICE is Nice and Chee Chee is Peachy."

South Pole Station circa 1974 as seen from the air

10 EPILOGUE

March 1974. MCB 71 was selected as the best Seabee battalion in the Navy and received the Peltier Award. The citation accompanying the Award reads: "…The officers and men of MCB 71 have greatly enhanced the image of the Seabees in the most remote corner of this earth and they can be justifiably proud of their achievements. Their performance has been of the highest caliber in every respect and they are considered most worthy of recognition as the Navy's best Mobile Construction Battalion during Fiscal Year 1974"

The main reason for this was we completed two years of construction in one year and in a small way I feel honored to be a part of that.

In addition the society of American Military Engineers announced that Steelworker Second Class Kenneth L. Welch had received the Marvin Shields award for his exceptional leadership in the performance of steel erection projects in McMurdo.

It was during this time the one of our Seabee brothers lost his life, BUCN Patrick J. Seely. I was told it was a freak accident he apparently came home one evening while on liberty and the vehicle he was driving slipped out of park and rolled over him. Chief Sunshine with 31 other members of the battalion made an eight hour bus trip (one way) to attend the funeral and say goodbye to our brother Bee.

12 April 1974. We said goodbye to our beloved LCDR William H. Kay, Jr. as he was transferred. It was during this time that we had an in ranks inspection with full medals for the change of command. We were giving Brillo a hard time and were asking him why he wasn't wearing his "Purple Penis Award."

20 April 1974. I was married to my Sweetheart Diane Campaneillo from Natick, Massachusetts in April with "Brillo" and Danks standing in for me at the Chapel in the pines in Davisville.

June 1974. I passed my Petty Officer Second Class exam that I had taken while I was at the South Pole and I was promoted. I was surprised and glad because I was a newlywed.

June 1974. I made one more deployment with MCB 71; this time to Bermuda with LCDR Gerard A. Zimmerman as commander, but it wasn't the same. We worked at night laying 2 inches of asphalt on an active runway that was both a civilian and military airfield. The runway was used during the day and new asphalt was laid at night. It was funny in Antarctica we worked solely during the day and now we were working solely at night.

14 February 1975. I rented a cottage in Bermuda and my first born daughter Claire was born there, Jimmy Grace acted as her Godfather.

Years later, I made contact with Jimmy who lived in the Baltimore area. He started his own construction company there and lives in a home he built on the Chesapeake Bay. Jimmy's son James L. Grace, Jr. is now a member of the Navy Seabees stationed in California. Jimmy stayed in the reserves and is a retired Chief Petty Officer.

June 1975. As part of an effort to save money Davisville was closed down and the Battalion was moved to Gulfport, Mississippi where we were later decommissioned after the deployment to Bermuda in 1975.

December 1985. The following article concerning Brillo appeared in the Wall Street Journal:

"MCMURDO STATION, Antarctica -- It was Saturday night at one of the world's most remote outposts, and Navy steelworker Barton "Brillo" was waving a bottle of high-octane Chilean liquor over his head. "I foresee adventure tonight," he shouts. The next day, after a sleepless night, he wanders glassy-eyed through the mess hall here, mumbling to himself.

Brillo's drinking binge ends Monday morning as he stares with bloodshot eyes into a coffee cup. "I can't look myself in the mirror anymore," says Brillo, who was 30 years old but appears to be 15 years older. "I drink too much."

Like many of the 1,000 U.S. sailors, scientists and others stationed here each year, Mr. Brillo loves the unspoiled wilderness, the challenging work and the camaraderie, but he hates the boredom and isolation. "We work ourselves to death," he says, tears welling up in his eyes. "Then we drink ourselves to death." (Burrough, 1985)

October 2007. MCB 71 was planning for a reunion and published a Newsletter for all veterans called the MCB Transit II announcing a reunion in August 2008 and had articles on our work and mentioned Brillo's award:

At battalion disestablishment, we turned over all our records to either COMCBLANT or COM20NCR. There are so many stories during my two-year assignment, many concern the accomplishments that we achieved resulting in our awards, but also many were comical ones either at the time or in retrospect. E.g., the first, and probably only, "Purple Penis" medal awarded by COMCBLANT to one of the battalion members on the Ice.

I had always thought that the Purple Penis Award that was given to Brillo was a joke, until years later; I happened to meet a naval communications officer that when I had mentioned I had been to the South Pole said, "Have you ever heard of the purple penis award." I said, *Yes? How do you know about it?* He said he was working in a shipboard communications center when the approval from the Secretary of the Navy for the purple penis award came through the com center. He said it was so amusing that he never forgot it.

December 2009. The station we had built had outlived its usefulness and was replaced by a new design that lifted the building up above the snow. As a result our wonderful dome was disassembled and was crated up and shipped back to the Seabee Museum in Port Hueneme where the crown was now on display along with the nuclear power panel which was removed from McMurdo. However, I am proud to say, the wonder arch that I and the other steelworkers constructed are still in use and holding up fine. According to Peter Rejcek, Antarctic Sun Editor:

> "It was never supposed to hang around this long. Ten years, maybe 15 at most. Perhaps that's why the South Pole Dome -- a modestly sized structure spanning 164 feet and topping out at about 52 feet high -- has loomed so large in the lore and legacy of polar history. The final chapter in that story will be completed 35 years after the U.S. Antarctic Program's most iconic research station was officially dedicated in January 1975. The dome, the second research station built at the geographic South Pole, was coming down.
> "That means [that] icon will no longer be there, and it's really sad to know that it's coming down, and I won't be there this year to be part of it," said Jerry Marty.

A longtime Polie (as South Pole residents are called), Marty retired earlier this year from the National Science Foundation (NSF) after devoting the last 15 years of his life to the construction of the third and latest South Pole Station. He had also been involved in the final year of construction on the station during the 1974-75 season, mainly attending to the last-minute fixes before the first crew moved in that January.

The new station, a two-story structure built atop stilts on a moving ice sheet, officially entered into service on Jan. 12, 2008. But even before then the geodesic dome, erected by U.S. Mobile Construction Battalion 71 (the Seabees), had been relieved of duty.

Civilian construction crews had finished disassembling the modular buildings under the protective aluminum shell a couple of winters ago after all operations had moved to the elevated station. More recently, the dome had been used for cold storage. Completion of a new logistics facility, an arched building near the elevated station, over this past winter means all those frozen goods now have a dedicated warehouse for storage.

The dome, half buried by drifted snow and empty of everything but memories must go as part of the South Pole long-term modernization plan.

Navy Seabees built the first South Pole Station during a frenzy of scientific activity known as the International Geophysical Year (IGY). A global effort of research during 1957-58, IGY particularly focused on the polar regions. The United States eventually built seven research stations to support scientists for their work in Antarctica.

Navy Seabees assembled the first South. Pole Station in less than two months over the 1956-57 field season for what was to be a temporary science campaign. In reality, IGY never really ended. And no one had predicted the collection of hastily built

Jamesway tents and connecting tunnels would need to last nearly 20 years.

Snow quickly buried the first station, commonly referred to as Old Pole. Eventually, the crushing weight of the snow on the ice-entombed structures meant time was running out before the station would become uninhabitable.

The Navy Facilities Engineering Command had determined that a new design was required for continued research by the National Science Foundation at the South Pole, according to a 1977 document published by the dome design and manufacture company, Temcor of Torrance, Calif.

A dome "would be large enough to enclose and protect three buildings for quarters and operations, two of them two stories high. All these buildings were supported above the snow floor of the dome for cross ventilation," wrote Temcor vice president Don L. Richter in the 1977 dome design document.

"The dome was to offer shelter from the wind and snow, but not the cold. The need was to keep the inside temperature below 0 [degrees] F to prevent deformation of the snow support and settlement destruction of the buildings. Five vent holes were opened in the top of the dome to bleed off warm air."

Lee Mattis was the Temcor project engineer who designed the specialized erection equipment and the scheme of how to build a geodesic dome on ice. "I was the guy who said, 'OK, here's the dome, but here's how we're going to put it up,'" said Mattis, who spent two seasons at South Pole during the dome construction between 1971 and 1973.

Why a dome? Mattis said a dome was a very efficient structure in terms of stability and the protection it offers from the snow. "The problem was the snow build-up [with Old Pole]. They felt if they could keep the snow off the buildings, they could extend the life, and that turned out to be true.

"The dome was a unique structure. It was very strong. It has a low profile," added Mattis, who returned to the South Pole in 2005 to advise the NSF about possible ways to bring the dome safely down. Going up and putting up the dome certainly wasn't an easy task in the brief Antarctic summer, where ambient temperatures rarely reach 0 degrees Fahrenheit. The foundation proved to be the trickiest part because a crucial piece of machinery couldn't handle the harsh conditions.

The Seabees used a Peter Snow Miller, a Swiss snowplow used to clear roads in the Alps, to process the snow and work it up to the firmness necessary to support the dome's wooden foundation footings. The same machine did double-duty in cutting a circular trench for the dome foundation and a trench for the "utilidor" for utility and sewage lines.

The hydraulic machine constantly broke down and was "always a mess," Mattis recalled. "The Peter Snow Miller was a major problem." He said little of the dome actually went up in 1971-72.

Most of the erection occurred the following season, 1972-73. "Basically, we went back down and did it," Mattis said.

During this time, the Seabees were also busy constructing a new power plant and arches to serve as a garage. Work on these structures and the interior dome buildings continued into the 1973-74 and 1974-75 seasons. Civilian contractors, including Marty, with the company Holmes and Narver Inc., mainly worked on the utilities.

On Jan. 9, 1975, a group of dignitaries dedicated the new station, including Ruth Siple, wife of Paul Siple, the first South Pole winter-over leader in 1957.

Bill Spindler worked as the South Pole station manager for a year in 1976-77, during the dome's third year in service, and has been involved with the U.S. Antarctic program on and off for more than 30 years. An engineer by trade, Spindler also wintered twice more, in 2005 and 2008.

The unofficial historian of the South Pole, Spindler was matter-of-fact when asked about its imminent disassembly.

"When I showed up at Pole in 1976, the dome made the new station seem state-of-the-art," he wrote in an e-mail. "No more collapsing snow tunnels, lots of storage space, and an instant icon for the U.S. Antarctic Research Program.

"But snow happens, things get old, drifts build up and structures get stressed," he added. "As an engineer, my feeling at this point was that the dome has outlived its usefulness at Pole and needs to go away before it becomes a structural hazard." Time to go

During the late 1980s, the NSF started preliminary planning for a new station, and at the time, the dome was sacrosanct, according to Spindler. "All plans for the new station included it, either as a cover for buildings, as it was in the existing station, a storage space, or perhaps even an insulated and heated structure. Some of the designs even included building another dome to match the original.

"All of this suddenly was to change as a result of a loud noise heard by the 1988 winter-overs," he explained. "They reported that it sounded like something broke."

A computer analysis at about the same time indicated that some of the aluminum dome foundation base ring beams might be overstressed, Spindler said. "The next summer the entire base ring was dug out, and yours truly got to crawl through the trench and inspect every node and every beam. Sure enough, I found cracks and broken beams at the predicted locations."

The damage was repaired, but the dream of keeping the dome in some capacity was broken. The winning design would call for a 65,000-square-foot building capable of sleeping about 150 people, elevated above the polar plateau and capable of being jacked up twice during its lifetime.

The Antarctic Treaty, an international agreement among nations with scientific interests and operations in Antarctica, requires obsolete structures like the dome to be removed where practicable.

The dome would have to go. But how?

In 2005, to assess how the dome could be deconstructed, Mattis said he returned to the South Pole at the behest of the Navy Civil Engineering Corps (CEC)/Seabee Historical Foundation, which would like to save the dome for posterity.

What did he think after seeing the dome for the first time in more than 30 years? "My first thought was, 'wow.' Why did I become a civil engineer? Because I wanted to see what I built, and here was something that lasted for much longer than it was designed to last. It's still functional. It's still working. It's still providing its intended use. It was a feeling of pride. Just to go back and see it was great," Mattis said.

"It was in good shape," he added. His recommendation to disassemble the dome was basically to reverse the order of construction -- taking it apart from the top down. Coming down

That's pretty much the plan, according to Brandon "Shaggy" Neahusan, construction manager for Raytheon Polar Services Co. (RPSC) and the lead person for the deconstruction project. RPSC was the prime contractor to the NSF for the U.S. Antarctic Program. RPSC's crew also built the new $150 million station over the past decade.

"The overall method we will be using was to start at the top and peel it like an orange," Neahusan said via-email from Antarctica. "In other words, we start at the top and move around the dome, panel by panel, clockwise disassembling until we get to the foundations."

The job -- which also includes taking down Skylab, a separate, orange, boxy tower that housed different science experiments near the dome -- will require a six-person crew.

First, the piece to be removed will be rigged to a crane and then two people working from a lift will use abrasive saws from the inside of the dome to cut partially through the structural members. Once that team was safely out of the way, a second two-person team working from the exterior of the dome will finish cutting the piece free. The crane will then lower the pieces to the ground, where the other two workers will continue to disassemble the panels for eventual transport from South Pole by plane or tractor train.

Neahusan said the primary challenge for such a job was safety. "Demolition was inherently dangerous work, so we take every action possible to mitigate the risks associated with it," he said. "This was a handpicked crew that I've worked with for several seasons now, and as this was a very high-profile project, it's my responsibility to not let my crew feel any of that pressure and just allow them to do their jobs."

Time and weather are the other obstacles. The project started in mid-November by clearing out the dome and moving snow away from outside perimeter for the heavy equipment to operate. Temperatures need to remain above minus 40 degrees Fahrenheit for the cranes and mechanical lifts to work properly -- not always a guarantee, even in summer.

"We plan to have both buildings down and packaged for shipment off continent by end of season," Neahusan said. For posterity

The crown of the dome and the next two rows of polygonal panels will be saved for display at a new Seabee museum in Port Hueneme, Calif.

"Disassembly will be accomplished by removing the bolted connections and using a tool called a collar cutter to snip the heads off the existing rivets and removing each component of the dome, documenting it for reassembly and crating the components for shipment to Port Hueneme," Neahusan said. "The rest of the structure will be cut up and shipped off continent and be recycled."

Neahusan said that the NSF had tried to figure out a way to send the whole dome back to the United States for display at the Seabee museum or other locations interested in its history. However, the labor costs alone would have been six times more expensive, and "the amount of time it would take to do so would not fit into the Congressionally mandated end date of the South Pole Station Modernization effort, which was March 31st, 2010."

Marty, who has been working with the CEC/Seabee Historical Foundation the last few years on bringing the dome to Port Hueneme, said the entire dome likely wouldn't fit in the new museum based on its current configuration.

"It's the old story of when you start to put things in a museum, it fills up pretty quick," he said. The new museum's concept was to suspend the dome near an exhibit focused on the polar history of the Seabees, according to Marty.

The current museum, converted from two Quonset huts, displays various Antarctic artifacts, such as a 4-foot by 8-foot sheet of plywood with braided rope around the edges. The Seabees who built the dome burned their names into the wood, which a forklift tine had damaged at some point. A demolition crew discovered the memento while taking apart the buildings under the dome, Marty said.

The new museum itself will be a "virtual" walk through of Seabee history. Visitors will follow in the Seabee' footsteps, starting with basic training and then on to conflicts from World War II and the Korean War to Vietnam and the modern conflicts in the Middle East. Finally, the tour ends with a look into their humanitarian and civil projects.

"The military campaigns are one thing, but the Seabees are unique because they've got this Antarctic-IGY piece of their historical background," Marty noted.

It would seem the dome was no longer for Polies alone.

"I think it hit us harder when we saw the galley and all the buildings inside go away," said Doug "Dog" Forsythe, a RPSC construction manager involved in the construction of the new station from the beginning in the late 1990s. "I hate to see it go, but I guess that's progress." (Rejcek, 2009)

Dome and New South Pole-Wonder Arch was buried

BIBLIOGRAPHY

Anon., 1973 . *American Presidency Project: Richard Nixon: Proclamation 4255 - Thanksgiving Day,*. [Online]
Available at:
http://www.presidency.ucsb.edu/ws/index.php?pid=72479#ixzz1kpTuae00
[Accessed 29 January 2012].

Anon., 1974. A Southern Christmas. *The Transit*, January, p. 3.

Anon., 1999-2011. *Urban Dictionary.* [Online]
Available at:
http://www.urbandictionary.com/define.php?term=midrats
[Accessed 23 January 2012].

Anon., 2006. *http://wonderbuilding.com/wb_history.html.* [Online]
[Accessed 20 January 2012].

Anon., 2007. *MCB 71.com.* [Online]
Available at:
http://www.mcb71.com/SPRING%202007.wpd%20color%20heading.pdf
[Accessed 14 February 2012].

Anon., 2010. *Alcoa Fasten Systems.* [Online]
Available at: http://www.afshuck.net/en/How_Huck_Works.html
[Accessed 26 January 2012].

Anon., 2012. *Omaha's orginal gi surplus.* [Online]
Available at: http://www.omahas.com/usaf-issue-mukluks
[Accessed 27 January 2012].

Anon., n.d. *Dry Gulch, Antarctica.* [Online]
Available at:

http://www.southpolestation.com/trivia/drygulch/drygulch.html
[Accessed 24 January 2012].

Burrough, B., 1985. Seeing 'Cat Ballou' 87 Times. *Wall Street Journal*, 10
12.

Fogle, B., 2011. *Mail Online.* [Online]
Available at: http://www.dailymail.co.uk/home/moslive/article-
1374428/Ben-Fogle-finds-inspiration-Scotts-Antarctic-base-
camp.html
[Accessed 26 January 2012].

Fr. F. X. Shouppe, S. J., 1973. *Purgatory.* Rockford: Tan Books.

Gannon, R., 1974. PS visits dome-covered "Science City" at the South Pole.
Popular Science, May, p. 76.

Lewis, R. S., 1966. *A Continent for Science.* New York: Viking Press.

Meloy, J. R. G. C., 1994. *Rorschach Assessment of Aggressive and
Psychopathic Personalities.* Mahwah: Lawrence Erlbaum
Associates.

Navy, U., n.d. Support for Science-Antarctica. *US Navy Publication, History
and Research Division*, p. 23.

Rejcek, P., 2009. *On Orbit Alpha.* [Online]
Available at: http://www.onorbit.com/node/1797
[Accessed 8 Feburary 2012].

Tennyson, A. L., 1842. *"Ulysses" Poem.* s.l.:s.n.

ABOUT THE AUTHOR

It has been almost 40 years since I last stepped foot on the Continent of Antarctica. It was a turning point in my life. Since that day in early February 1974 I have never forgotten it. I still continue as Lord Alfred Tennyson said, "To Strive, To Seek, To Find, and not to Yield. After returning to Davisville R.I., I married my sweetheart and fathered seven children; two boys and five girls and I have four grandchildren. Below are photos of my eldest son and grandson pointing at my name on the plaque we left at the South Pole. It is now in the Seabee museum in Port Hueneme, California. After the ICE, I spent three more years in the Navy and make a deployment to Bermuda with MCB 71 and was stationed afterward in Sigonella, Sicily. I then joined the Army Military Police Corps. I often would joke the Seabees taught me to steal and in the Army taught me how to catch a thief. I eventually retired from the Army making the rank of Chief or Sergeant First Class. I am a student of life. I am a graduate from the University of Maryland and have a Master's degree from Northern Arizona University and I am currently working on obtaining my Doctorate from Grand Canyon University. I am an avid hiker and I currently live in the Sedona, Arizona area.

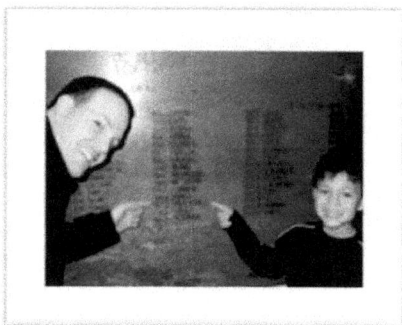

www.ingramcontent.com/pod-product-compliance
Lightning Source LLC
Chambersburg PA
CBHW070524030426
42337CB00016B/2099